Neversink

Neversink

ONE ANGLER'S INTENSE EXPLORATION OF
A TROUT RIVER

Leonard M. Wright, Jr.

THE ATLANTIC MONTHLY PRESS
NEW YORK

Published simultaneously in Canada
Printed in the United States of America

Library of Congress Cataloging-in-Publication Data

Wright, Leonard M.
Neversink: one angler's intense exploration of a trout river / Leonard M. Wright, Jr.
ISBN 0-87113-502-7
1. Trout fishing—New York (State)—Neversink River.   2. Fly fishing—New York
(State)—Neversink River.   3. Natural history—New York (State)—Neversink River.
4. Neversink River (N.Y.)
I. Title   SH688.U6W75   1991   799.1'755—dc20   91-21790

Design by Laura Hough

The Atlantic Monthly Press
19 Union Square West
New York, NY 10003

FIRST PRINTING

Go softly by that riverside, or when you would depart,
you'll find its ever winding tied and knotted round your heart.

—RUDYARD KIPLING

Contents

FOREWORD xi

1 INTO THE VALLEY 1

2 THE LAY OF THE WATER 13

3 *Fontinalis* 23

4 THE BAD OLD DAYS 37

5 "LET US NOW PRAISE . . ." 49

6 *Trutta* 55

7 ENEMIES 65

8 THE LIFE BLOOD 71

9 THE WAY OF A STREAM 81

10 THE HIGH COST OF OVERHEAD 89

11 GLORIOUS FOOD 99

Contents

12 SIDE ORDERS 111

13 FOOD OF THE FOOD 119

14 "LET THERE BE LIGHTS . . ." 127

15 ". . . AND THERE WAS LIGHTS" 137

16 *Salar Sebago* 141

17 BESIDE THE STILL WATERS 153

18 WIND AND WEATHER 161

19 GREEN THINGS 165

20 THE BIRDS AND THE BEASTS 171

21 THE ONCE AND FUTURE RIVER 183

Foreword

What you are about to read is not a fish story although, I'll admit, parts of it are distinctly fishy. After all, it was the trout that attracted me to this river in the first place and then led me to explore, study, and finally write about it. Still, the fish are only supporting characters. The heroes in this tale are the river itself and, inseparably, the Neversink Valley that creates and sustains it.

And although this story is a true one, it is only that—not a hard-science tract. I have no degree in biology or in any associated ecological sciences, so this book will not follow the usual scientific methods. Instead, it concentrates on those aspects of a river that I was most curious about, and I can only hope they're the ones you'll find most interesting, too.

Generally, the sequence of events or discoveries progresses as my own observations and learning did—starting with the fish, moving on to the water they live in, the fish foods this river produces, and so on back to more remote, yet contributing, influences. In other words, rather than starting with the fundamentals of a river system and progressing up the food chain to its top link, I will proceed mainly in the opposite direction, as my personal inquiries did.

Don't expect coverage of the entire river system, either. That, too, would stretch my experience because, in a very real sense, a river never begins or ends. Its true sources are destabilizing air masses thousands of miles from its watershed. After the resulting raindrops have fallen within its basin, and traveled from trickle to brook, to stream, to river, to estuary, they wind up as faint traces in ocean currents that only the homing salmon can sniff out.

I am limiting this story to the one relatively short portion of the Catskill's Neversink River that I know intimately, from the point where large brooks join up to create a stream and on down to where, as a small river, the Neversink flattens out into a reservoir. During this twelve miles of travel, the river loses over five hundred feet in elevation in a sequence of rapids, flats, runs, and pools. Typically, most of this descent occurs in the river's upper reaches. The last five miles of main-stem river, below the junction of its two branches, drops little more than 150 feet.

Even in this lower portion, the river is exceptionally clear and cold. In a deep pool you can easily make out individual pebbles on the bottom in ten feet of water. It is no river for swimmers. Water temperatures rarely reach the comfort point of 70 degrees even on the hottest midsummer afternoons.

No major events in history have taken place in the upper Neversink Valley. George Washington never hurled so much as a penny across its waters, not even in legend. No battles, and not even a skirmish with the local Indians, ever took place here.

And yet to fly-fishers it is a river steeped in history. The revered Theodore Gordon created American dry-fly fishing and fly patterns on its waters. Later, on the very same stretch of river, Edward R. Hewitt pioneered and popularized trout fishing with underwater nymph imitations.

To nonanglers, an exploration of this river may offer a slightly different appeal. The chain of life-forms it nurtures and the laws of hydrology that rule it make up one of the least-known yet most absorbing stories in the entire field of natural history.

Although the Neversink differs slightly from other rain-fed rivers in its temperature, configuration, clarity, volatility, and fertility, the networks of animal and vegetable life it produces, and the intricate ways it does so, are identical. Understand how and why one cold-water river works and you're on intimate terms with the hundreds of others that make up the majority of our running-water trout fisheries.

For over two decades now I have drunk from it, fished it, studied it, and struggled to improve it. I have examined it every month of the year, charting changes in its streambed and looking into the numbers, types, and habits of the life-forms it produces. I have also scoured libraries and questioned biologists and hydrologists to learn more about running waters in general and this one in particular. It is an exercise that never ends: I am still learning and discovering.

The result, then, while perhaps not an *Odyssey*, is at least a travelogue—an account of a journey toward understanding. Some destinations may seem blurry. There are few triumphant arrivals. As with most trips, the act of traveling itself provided most of the suspense and excitement.

I should add here that my life was not as tightly focused on the river as this book might lead you to believe. I am not a member of that honored British métier, the full-time, professional river keeper. During the period covered here, I have a wife, three children, and a five-day-a-week job in New York City—to mention just a few of the other minor demands on my time and attention.

Studying and tinkering with this river fishery has been only a hobby then, though an absorbing one. In fact, I have become so engrossed in it that if I leave the river for a week's salmon fishing in Canada, or even a day's shad fishing on the nearby Delaware River, guilt gnaws at me. Would that be the week when there'd be hatches of a mayfly species I'd never noted before? Might that be the one evening of the season when truly large trout fed on the surface? Could I afford to squander all that precious free time when I was so far behind on river-improvement projects?

Friends who've noticed this preoccupation have said, "You're really in love with that river, aren't you?"

I always consider that question rhetorical, not requiring a yes or no. Anyway, I could only reply to it in much the way one of my own questions was once answered.

When I was far younger, I asked a woman, who had enjoyed forty years of what everyone considered a perfect marriage, whether or not she was still in love with her husband. I was probably out of line, but we were close friends and she had a reputation for utter frankness.

"What an odd question." There was a long pause before she continued. "Despite what everyone thinks, it hasn't been all peaches and cream. He's not perfect, you know, and neither am I. Oh, I was gaga over him when we got married, all right. These days it's all so different. He's been such an enormous part of my life for so many years that by now I can't imagine what, or even who, I would be without him. What would you call that?"

What indeed? I'll admit that I was infatuated with the river during my first seasons in the Valley—even though it, too, was far from perfect. It seldom produced the glut of flies or rising trout that fishermen dream about. I have found it frequently ungenerous, often frustrating, sometimes almost malevolent.

Yet what it lacks in quantity it makes up for in quality. Because of its pure, icy, fast water, its trout are exceptionally strong, elegantly formed, rock-firm to the touch, and superb eating. Then, too, they live in a picturesque river that runs through an unspoiled valley. For all its shortcomings, the Neversink has become "my river" and if I were exiled to another—even a far more productive one—I'm sure I'd feel that some part of myself were missing.

1

Into the Valley

Last May I managed to lose the biggest trout I have ever hooked on a dry fly in the Neversink or in any other eastern river. I still can't decide whether the escape was due to poor handling or bad luck, but in either event, this is how it happened.

It was a cloudy, but not threatening, afternoon near the end of the month, and I had been methodically covering likely water with a Grey Fox Variant—a high-floating, grayish-brown pattern with a hackle collar nearly the size of a silver dollar. It's a pattern I've found successful when I'm trying to convince nonrising fish that such a big mouthful is worth a round trip to the surface. I'd been out for an hour without much success and was beginning to lose my concentration when conditions took a sharp turn for the better. I began to see big brown mayflies on the surface, and in a few minutes a fair hatch of them was in progress.

I had just reached the tail of a favorite pool and stopped there to watch for the swirls or expanding circles that would betray the positions of fish feeding upstream. I thought I saw a disturbance up near the throat of the pool and was about to move up to investigate when, only a dozen feet away, a shape materialized out of nowhere, glided upward, sucked a fly off the surface and sank back down into invisibility again. The fish was angled away from me during this maneuver so I couldn't estimate his length, but he looked a good three inches thick across the shoulders and was clearly a brute.

Fearing the fish might spot me at such close range I backed off several feet and waited for another appearance so I could get accurate bearings on his lie. A minute later he rose a second time and gave me a full side view. He was pale tan with enormous spots and he was at least twenty inches long.

Since I recognized the flies on the water as Grey Foxes, my variant imitation of that natural seemed a reasonable choice, and after checking my leader-tippet for wind-knots I decided to stay with it. I moved slightly downstream and farther out into the river to get a better casting angle. When I was all set, I cast my fly three feet above him and watched it inch downcurrent toward me. After my second pitch I realized I was panting violently, and started making a conscious effort to keep my breathing normal.

A half minute later the fish tilted up again and took a natural less than a foot from my imitation. This convinced me that my pattern wasn't realistic enough so I waded ashore to fumble through my fly box. I finally found a standard Grey Fox dressing and compared it to my variant. The hackle and tails were the same color, but the variant, tied on a short-shank hook, had only a hint of body. The dressing on the standard hook, on the other hand, sported a succulent yellow body a good half-inch long. If the fish wasn't interested in wings, which the long hackles of the variant imitated beautifully, perhaps he was tuning in to the meaty abdomens.

This turned out to be a good hunch, for the trout took the new pattern on the second cast and, when he felt the hook, raced up the pool. I could have stopped a hundred-pound tarpon just as easily, and when the run ended it was the fish's decision not mine. He had pulled into a sanctuary—an undercut in the cliff that formed the far side of the pool—and decided he was now out of harm's way.

I could still feel the throb of the fish's slow swimming, but I could also feel my leader grating against the rock shelf and knew I had to get him out of there. To spare my leader, I eased up to light pressure and moved upstream to get opposite the fish, reeling in my line as I went.

When I got across stream from him I increased the pressure a bit to let the fish know that the invisible pull that was plaguing him had followed him into his refuge. I can't believe that fish was thinking what I was thinking; still, in a minute or so, he swam out and headed down the pool. He wasn't running as fast now, and as he neared the tail of the pool he evidently thought better of the shallower water and headed back up toward me.

By this time he was nearly beaten and would make only short, boring spurts toward the bottom with two or three consecutive thrusts of his tail before line pressure started pulling him up toward the surface again. When he came to the top and stayed there, just wagging his tail, I reached for my net. And at that moment, my leader flipped up and back over my head.

My first thought was that the hook had pulled free because I wasn't exerting anything like the pull needed to pop that four-pound-test leader. There was no fly on the end, though, and the tippet was roughened from abrasion in at least two places. I don't think that fish had any idea of how lucky he had been.

Fed up with fishing for the moment, I sat down on a rock to mull things over. It struck me that those last five minutes were actually a synopsis or a miniature of my life on the river: a series of exhilarating highs punctuated by crushing disappointments.

My first encounter with the upper Neversink had definitely not been one of those high points. Though it was common knowledge that the lower river had been nearly ruined by a dam that choked off most of the flow, the pristine and private water above was reputed to be a sparkling jewel.

On the day my wife and I first drove into that valley over twenty years earlier, my expectations were soaring. When a ribbon of water suddenly appeared off to my left, I pulled over onto the shoulder and got out for a closer look at what I hoped would be my new river.

My first reaction was that it was smaller than I had anticipated. It had so often been paired with the neighboring Beaver Kill that I had always visualized the Neversink as the same size as the Beaver Kill's main stem after it had been joined by the Willowemoc below the town of Roscoe. Instead, this river was only about half as large—some thirty feet wide in the runs and swelling out to fifty feet or more in the pools.

Even more disappointing, it looked black and sullen. I climbed down to the water's edge for a closer look. The strange color, I saw, was due to a dark blue algae that clung to the rocks like ugly hanks of hair. It looked like a slime you'd expect to see in a badly polluted stream. Being a fair-weather angler, I'd never seen this growth before and had no idea that the algae was a common cold-water plant that disappeared quickly once the water warmed up.

All in all, it wasn't a case of even moderate affection at first sight.

Though it was nearly May, the death of the past year still gripped the surrounding countryside. During the two-hour, 110-mile drive northwest from the George Washington Bridge, we had traveled from lush, full spring back into stark, winter conditions. The crab apple and cherry trees we passed on our way out the Henry Hudson Parkway had already blossomed, dropped their petals, and were in full summer leaf. But up here, in the high Catskills, the shrubs and trees were winter-naked and the fields showed only a hint of green.

As we drove further upvalley, the river disappeared, looping off behind tree-lined fields, then reappeared a half mile beyond. This second coming did nothing to improve my impression of the water.

As we entered the hamlet of Claryville, I turned left, as instructed, crossed two bridges in quick succession, then took the next left up a small dirt road. Here the woods suddenly opened up into a five-acre clearing, complete with house, garage, and a car parked out front.

We were met at the door by a tall, angular woman in her seventies, who welcomed us cordially and showed us around the house. Completely done over by the previous owner, the interior of the place was far more elegant than its boxy farmhouse exterior had suggested.

I'd heard about this property a month earlier from a friend who was close to the owner's family and had been offered the place for rental. Since he was not a fisherman, he had little interest in a house in such an out-of-the-way area. But knowing I was an ardent angler, he suggested I write the owner and mention his name.

He told me she already owned five miles of valley and river directly upstream, and that when this place came on the market she'd picked it up to "protect her flank." She had no immediate use for the property, but felt that someone should enjoy it. When I learned of this vast holding, I nicknamed her, sight unseen, "The Queen of the West Branch"—the Queen, for short—and in my family that honorific has stuck to her—used, of course, only when she was not present.

During our house tour she explained that the bottom mile of the West Branch ran through the property, which included 250 acres of deer and grouse cover extending up the hill behind the house. She mentioned, with some hesitancy, a modest rental price and asked if we were interested. I still wonder why she bothered to ask—at that price, of course we were.

"Well, then, that's settled," she said. "You can move in as soon as you like. The caretaker will pick up the garbage every Monday and mow the lawns as he has been." Then, as an afterthought, "I'm not sure this stretch of water is particularly good, so I'll allow you fishing privileges on the next mile just above, as well." And that was it. There was no lease, just the verbal agreement. Never before or since have I been treated with such instant acceptance and benevolence. I kept

telling myself that things like this happened only in Victorian novels—
if, in fact, they ever happened at all.

She then asked if I'd brought any tackle and seemed pleased when
I admitted that I had. The moment she left I strung up my rod, put on
boots and vest, and loped across the short meadow to the river.

Directly below the house lay a long, inviting pool. Because of its
proximity to the house, it became known as "Home Pool." Its waters
that day were high and frigid, but clear. I tried dry fly, wet fly,
streamer—everything I could think of short of worms—but got not a
touch. Nor did I see any sign of fish or fly life. The river proved to be
as dead as it looked, and after a full hour of flogging I returned to the
house chilled and letdown. Was this water as poor as my new landlady
had suspected, after all?

Commitments confined us to the city the following weekend, and
by the time we moved in, during mid-May, the Valley had been
transformed. Fields were as green as Ireland, the shadbush and cherries
were in full blossom, and white buds were starting to burst on the apple
trees.

The river, too, had undergone a mysterious change. Its stones had
shed their black slime and turned a warm, golden brown. Rapids wore
lace in the sunshine.

After lunch, that first Saturday, I set up my rod, slipped into my
boots and headed for Home Pool. My fishing diary for that day
cryptically notes:

> "Day sunny, breezy, up to 60 degrees. Water height, medium
> . . . temp. 51 at 1:30. Fished Q.G. [Quill Gordon] dry. Ten brookies,
> four better than 9". Five browns, three 9", one 12", one 13". Quit
> at 4:30 when hatch stopped."

I don't really need that prompting, though. I still remember that
first good day on the Neversink in living color.

The first half hour went slowly. I raised only one smallish fish and at the last instant he disliked something about my offering and came short. Then mayflies with dark, Marconi-rigged wings began popping up near the head of the pool, coasting a dozen feet or more before taking off. Soon I noticed surface swirls in that area and hurried on up there.

My first five fish were all brook trout and mostly little ones. Finally I began to see rise forms that showed some authority, and by picking out the larger disturbances I began hooking into a better class of trout, including two brookies that crowded the ten-inch mark.

Typically, the largest trout didn't come on the feed until the hatch was nearly over, and the final two, both brown trout, were by far the best of the day. The last and largest one was feeding up in the choppy run that entered the pool and I would have missed him if I hadn't caught a flick of water out of the corner of my eye.

I moved upcurrent, floated the fly over his lie, and he came up at the first pitch, throwing water with his tail and hooking himself as he dove back down to the stream bottom. He raced off downstream, pulling line off the spool, and then settled down to slug it out in the belly of the pool, which was probably his usual residence. He treated me to two clean jumps and several strong runs before he let me net him.

I know some spring-creek anglers in the West who wouldn't waste a cast on a trout of only thirteen inches, but on an eastern freestone stream, browns of that size are coin of the realm. Such a trout is three years old, sexually mature, and is the staple "good fish" in the Beaver Kill and other Catskill fisheries. A fifteen-incher is a truly "big one" on all local rivers, except perhaps on the main-stem Delaware.

The pool went dead after that last capture, so I picked up my three good brookies and two fine browns, strung them by the gills on the fingers of my left hand, and marched proudly up to the house.

My first harsh judgment of the river was instantly repealed.

The following morning I set out to get on closer terms with my newly-admired river and its surroundings. I drove up the West Branch until it became a small brook, then reconnoitered back downstream as far as I could to a point where the lower river veered away from the road and was unfollowable. I didn't learn much, though, because the river and the road parted company for such long stretches that I was limited to only intermittent glimpses.

While parking the car in the garage, I noticed a contour map tacked to the wall and stepped over for a bird's-eye view of the Neversink Valley. Someone had inked in the area covered by the reservoir that blocks the river two or three miles below where it parts company with the road. Starting at that point, and tracing its winding path back upstream, I estimated that there were only five miles of main-stem river before it forked into two branches just below Claryville.

Running my left and right index fingers up each, I saw that both the East and West branches were of about the same size and length, and that their courses ran northeasterly for thirteen miles, nearly parallel and never more than three or four miles apart. Their sources were even closer: Both started on neighboring faces of 4,204-foot Slide Mountain, the highest peak in the Catskills.

Over the next two or three weeks I made several more morning explorations, usually following the riverbank on foot for a closer look, but these outings in no way interfered with the more serious business of fishing. In the early weeks of the season, mornings are downtime. Aquatic insects and trout rising to them are rarely seen before the water has warmed after the overnight cool-off. The two or three hours right after lunch provide the best fishing time, and these first few weeks offer what may be the choicest fishing of the year. By summer, flies are fewer and the fish better educated, tempted to feed well only in the fading light of dusk.

I had been a fly-fishing fanatic for years, but up to this time there had always been an unsettling element of urgency in my trouting. I'd had to plan ahead, clear the calendar, make a special trip. That done, I felt driven—as I still do during salmon trips to Canada—to make every minute count, whether or not conditions or time of day seemed favorable. There had also been a territorial drive in me to stake out a choice position on a pool; often I would tediously homestead it for an hour or more before the evening take could be expected.

Now my grim determination to put in long, often hopeless, hours was no longer necessary. "My fish" would be waiting for me when I felt conditions had turned propitious and I didn't have to worry about other anglers beating me to a known hot spot. The caretaker checked for poachers a couple of times a day and the water was tightly posted.

For years I had chafed at those white "Posted!" signs. I rarely saw anyone fishing in posted areas when I drove by and felt that some rich dog in the manger—or, more likely, the son of one—was preventing me from fishing there out of pure malice. In my new situation, however, I was immediately convinced that posting was one of the triumphant concepts of modern man.

Of course we had to show off our new place to friends. On the weekends following our move we entertained a steady parade of guests, and all of them had to be treated to the local specialty: trout dredged in flour and crisply fried. This, incidentally, is the only way to prepare prime, wild trout. Save those elaborate sauces for the tasteless, tank-raised substitutes they sell in supermarkets. They only overpower and mask the delicate flavor of stream-bred fish.

Frying a trout is about as easy as boiling water, yet I'm amazed at how many cooks—even cookbooks—manage to botch it. I've read time and again about how fish were hustled from the stream, plopped quickly into a skillet loaded with fresh butter, and after five minutes of sizzling turned into a Lucullan feast. Every single one of those directions is dead wrong.

A few years back I'd wheedled the proper method out of a lady chef who served up the world's most delicious trout at a small hotel in the Cévennes Mountains of south-central France. She insisted one should never sauté a trout until rigor mortis had set in and relaxed again, a process which takes several hours. If the fish are too fresh, they'll burst apart the way *truites bleues* are expected to, lose their juices, which should be sealed in, and cook unevenly due to their deformed shape.

Butter is about the worst shortening you can use. It smokes and burns at too low a temperature. Trout, like wild game, should be treated to high heat. Madame had used peanut oil. American oils can't stand the heat the way French ones do, so I use bacon fat instead.

Lastly, five minutes of cooking time is a joke. Depending on fish size, twenty to twenty-five minutes is more like it. I may be only a so-so fly-fisher, but I pride myself on being the world's second-greatest trout cooker.

After showing off both my piscatorial and culinary prowess for a couple of months, I found filling the skillet difficult. There were still plenty of six- to eight-inch tiddlers around, but prime, nine- to sixteen-inch fish, several dozens of which had already been converted into *sautée munière*, were disturbingly scarce.

The next time the caretaker dropped by to mow the lawn, I asked him how the fishing upriver was holding up.

"No complaints," he said. "Fishing usually stays good all summer in this cold river. And there are just about as many trout now as there were in spring because most of the fishers up there throw their fish back."

Didn't they ever kill a fish?

"Oh, once in a while they'll keep a couple for breakfast, but mostly they toss 'em back. If they didn't, they'd have her pretty well cleaned out by now. Poachers will sure do that for you if you don't keep them off. They treat a stream like a fish market and kill everything they can lay their hands on."

I guessed I knew what that made *me*. I quickly changed the subject and skulked away as soon as I could to avoid embarrassing questions.

Obviously I had severely overharvested my fishery—a malfeasance I'd never even heard of before. When I had fished public waters, I usually kept several good fish—if I was lucky enough to catch them. My approach had been purely exploitive and I'd never considered the supply side of the equation. How many years had it taken to grow those trout? How many decent ones could a mile of river produce? How long would it take for young recruits to mature and fill up the thinned ranks? I'd always trusted the state hatchery trucks to take care of that problem, and if they didn't I'd just take my business elsewhere, to a better-stocked stream.

You may be able to increase your own catch by fishing in the next valley, but you can't move a fishery to greener pastures because it stays stubbornly in place. If you want your water to remain productive, you can prune it judiciously, but you can't pig out on it.

Gradually, I was becoming aware of some of the guidelines for fishery management. But I was certainly learning them the hard way.

2

The Lay of the Water

In an attempt to restore some scale to my trout population, I did what most state fish departments and private clubs do: I resorted to stocking. I ordered a few dozen rather expensive twelve- to thirteen-inch trout from a nearby hatchery, which promised to deliver them the following weekend.

The day before the truck was due I decided I ought to survey my water so that the fish could be placed in the most stress-free holding lies until they grew accustomed to life in the river. I knew from fishing experience that large trout liked the security of depth, overhead cover, or both, and that they preferred gentle currents to torrents. At the price I was paying, the fish were going to end up in the cushiest quarters I could find.

The best way to learn the secrets of a stream or small river is to get right into the middle of it with chest-waders and Polaroid glasses. I chose an hour near noon when the light would be brightest and began at the long riffle just above Junction Pool, wading slowly upstream and sticking to the center as long as depth permitted. When I'd reached the top of this knee-deep stretch, I had to rate it as nursery water. Young trout, those under eight inches, would hold and feed in water that thin, but not those that had achieved any seniority.

The curved pool directly above Junction Pool was another matter, though, and had often yielded sizable trout. The water in its slow belly was deeper than the top of my waders and contained several sub-merged boulders so large that I had to detour around them. With depth, cover, and slow water, this was prime territory.

Above it, the stream veered to the right and picked up speed in a long run. This, too, was studded with boulders and rock slabs that created swirls and small cascades of white water. Fine lies here for medium-sized, wild fish—especially in late spring and summer when trout spread out from their deep, slow, wintering holes.

The river then swung to the left, completing an S and bringing me back to the tail end of Home Pool. This had held good fish in the spring, but was getting too shallow for good holding lies now that stream levels had dwindled. Nowhere, now, was it quite waist-deep. However, it had one intriguing feature in its tail end—a huge, flat, slab of rock lay flush in the surrounding rubble in ten inches of quickening water. This formation was so unusual that it stuck in my memory.

After wading up a brief, steep riffle, I came upon a short plunge pool just below the only bridge across the West Branch. Its concrete abutments pinched the river in times of flood and this accelerated flow had scoured a deep, short hole, leaving only a few large boulders. Here was prime holding water in summer, though it might become too fast and turbulent in high water to act as a secure wintering hole.

Next came over a hundred yards of unproductive riffle before the valley floor briefly leveled out to create 150 feet of slow water. This I had to classify as a flat because with a maximum depth of two feet it wasn't deep enough to be called a pool. It had proved a likely spot for fish up to ten inches, but it was no place for that last pitch at dusk when you're hoping to cap your day with a fish of a pound or better.

The following stretch was a lengthy disappointment. For half a mile or more the river ran ramrod straight and was nearly featureless. Its current maintained a steady pace, never accelerating into a rapids or slowing into a flat. It did not contain enough large rocks to scour out pockets, and it had built up no diagonal gravel bars that might shunt the current toward one bank or the other and dig out a deeper trough.

At last, above this wasteland, the river essed again, creating a chain of four appealing short pools connected by brief, pockety runs.

Clearly, there were only two areas worth stocking: the bottom three pools of my leased portion, and the lower reaches of the "permission" water above. Other sections of the river may have contributed to the fishery, either as a nursery or a producer of insect food, but it was sobering to realize how short a yardage, out of over a mile of first-rate river, provided prime fish-holding lies.

The truck appeared on schedule the next day and I hopped in to point out the chosen pools, all but one of which, fortunately, lay within a hundred feet of the road. At each appointed spot we put several fish into oversized buckets half-filled with tank water and lugged them to the river's edge. There we held them tilted into the stream, letting water trickle in slowly so that the fish would not be shocked by a sudden change in temperature.

Though these fish were brown trout, they barely resembled the fish the stream produced. Their shape was bulkier and their fins much thicker. Even their color was different: Their top halves were distinctly green instead of brown, and their sides, far more heavily spotted than the natives', were off-white rather than buttercup yellow. Still, they seemed lively enough, and when finally poured into the river they all swam out toward the deep middle of the pool, swung head on into the current, and took up stations just off the bottom.

Now that the hatchery had solved my fish-population problem—or so I then thought—I turned my attention once again to the physical state of the river. Home Pool, a favorite place to end an evening's fishing because it was only a short stumble through the dark to the house, was my first concern. It would cease to hold even a few decent trout if its level dropped any lower, whereas a gain of a foot or more would probably restore its springtime bounty.

That flat slab at its tail end, where the channel of the river was pinched to twenty-five feet, kept popping back into my mind until I finally realized its value. If I could use it as a center-pin, I could build a simple log dam there out of tree trunks that were only half the width of the river—logs I could handle myself, on the cheap, without bringing in expensive, heavy machinery.

I have never been accused of being a compulsive manual laborer, but here was a work project to my liking. An inborn fascination with running water had led me early in life to play water games. I vividly remember putting on a yellow slicker and matching sou'wester when it rained and rushing out to play with the flows that ran down the ruts of our driveway. As a child of only six or seven I'd erect small dams of sticks, mud, and stones, backing up temporary pools. When these were overwhelmed, I'd take trowel or hoe to kink or divert the currents, creating a series of meanders, always changing projects and tactics as flows swelled or dwindled. It was a favorite, informal game.

However, the river at hand was no trickle and I realized that making it do my bidding would not be child's play. To carry out my project would take sound planning and sturdy materials.

First I went to a steep hillside upriver and felled four straight-trunked hemlocks that measured ten to twelve inches in diameter. I chose hemlock because I'd heard it was one of the few woods that could be alternately wet and dry over the years without rotting. I trimmed the branches and sawed eighteen- to twenty-foot logs from their butt ends. I then levered them downhill toward the river with a crowbar. On steeper pitches I sometimes managed a free skid of ten or twenty feet. On flatter sections, however, I was often reduced to a one-inch gain per sweaty pry, and I commiserated with the slaves who'd built the pyramids. Finally I rafted them through the pools and dragged them over gravel bars and assembled them at the appointed site.

There I log-cabin-cut one end of each log so that two could be morticed together to appear as one. Next I augered holes through the splice-cut ends and star-drilled a hole one inch in diameter and several inches deep into the central rock itself.

I floated a log across stream until it was perpendicular to the current with the far end well up on the bank and the other, flat-cut side up, with its drilled hole directly over the one in the rock. A strong steel dowel inserted downward through both holes pinned the log firmly in place. The identical process was repeated on the opposite side of the river, only that log was positioned flat-side down so it would nest into the first. This created the appearance of one thirty-foot-plus log lying athwart the current.

Then came the tedious job of digging trenches a foot or two deep that cut several feet into both riverbanks to level the logs and secure their ends. Lastly, the identical job of positioning and burying was performed with the second set of logs so that they lay directly on top of the first pair. By the time I had filled in the log-end trenches and ballasted them with large, protective rock slabs, I had used up four precious days of vacation to create a sturdy-looking barrier that was two logs high.

At quitting time that last day, I stood around to watch the new pool fill up. It was not to happen—in those minimal summer flows, the reduced head of water easily slipped through the gaps between the logs and the uneven streambed. After all that sweat and strain, I had managed to raise the water level only a measly two or three inches.

The following day, however, delivered one of the few pleasant surprises I have ever received from river work. The pool had deepened by nearly two feet and in some places was trickling over the tops of the logs. I'd had no inkling of how much organic matter a river transports even during minimum flows. Small branches, twigs, leaves, grass cuttings, and a wide assortment of flotsam had lodged in those leaky gaps, making the structure reasonably watertight.

Within a week a new crop of fish, both wild and stocked, had discovered this new Eden with its five-foot depths. My created pool was admired by passersby and fellow anglers alike, and I made plans to deepen other likely places—perhaps that long, shallow flat, upriver—the following season. At four days a pool, which might be cut to two with the help of a willing or coerced guest, I would soon have the most productive water on the entire river.

As I was revelling in the success of my ingenious, unconventional dam, doubts about the overall health of my fishery began to creep in from another quarter. I was beginning to question the benefits of my recent stocking. Certainly it had restored some sizable trout to the water, but the fish themselves were synthetic and disappointing. Since they were used to regular handouts, they wallowed up to take almost any fly I put over them—especially those flies that resembled Purina fish pellets. This diet was also responsible for their soft white flesh, which had little flavor. And the coddled, tank environment had turned out flabby fighters.

Not only had a month of river life failed to smarten and harden them up, they began disappearing, and the stay-at-homes showed signs of losing weight and turning darker. After the first freshet in late August, a rise of less than three feet, only a few of my stock remained in my water.

I phoned an acquaintance who was a professional fishery consultant and described the situation. He wasn't encouraging.

"What did you expect? Hatchery fish have been genetically altered through generations of selective breeding. To get trout with a high survival rate in crowded tanks, you have to breed out wild characteristics like shyness, territoriality, and God knows what else.

The resulting domesticated strain survives fairly well in lakes and ponds where the living is easy, but life expectancy in fast-water streams is maybe two months. And don't expect to see any at all next spring—they just aren't equipped to make it through the tough times of winter."

I asked him why, with that dim a track record, stocking was such a widespread practice.

"Greed. Everybody, including the state, wants twice as many fish in a given stretch of water as it could naturally produce or support. And they don't mind in the least if they're easy to catch. Paying for put-and-take, short-lived hatchery fish is the only way they've found to do it."

That wasn't the end of it. I noticed that the big new fish hogged the best lies—the feed lanes where insect food was most concentrated. Territorial dominance in trout is bestowed by sheer size. There are no small, feisty heroes. A twelve-inch fish will intimidate an eleven-and-a-half-incher every time.

How was this crowding-out affecting the mostly smaller, wild fish? Were they getting enough leftovers to grow up to sporting size next season? Were they even accumulating enough reserves to make it through the deadly, food-short winter?

Nobody could provide accurate answers. But common sense told me that stocking was like addiction. The more you did it, the more you *had* to do it. The larger domestics would drive away or starve out the rising generations of wild trout until they were reduced to token numbers. I made a solemn promise that no matter how much the fishery appeared to be hurting, I would never again stock it with domestic fish.

By now it was early September, the last month of the open season, and I was beginning to think about grouse and woodcock, whose season opened the day after trout fishing closed. I may have been nearly finished with river matters for that year, but the river wasn't finished with me.

In late October came the day that I'd known might eventually arrive, but which I had lulled myself into believing might be several years off. The tail end of a hurricane roared up the coast, dropped torrents of rain for a full day, and raised the river a good six feet. When I arrived the following weekend, it took all the courage I could muster to walk down to the river to inspect my dam. There wasn't a vestige of it left, not even the hefty steel rod.

I stood there a long while, trying to reconstruct, step-by-step, the destruction of my dam. I finally remembered that there was always an awesome, blue plunge pool directly below any dam. And what created this? Huge volumes of water falling nearly vertically off the lip in floodtime had the power to blast out a deep trench, sluicing away all but the biggest boulders.

Once I was aware of this phenomenon I could easily pinpoint the inherent weakness in my structure. The heavy head of water, plunging downward over my logs, had excavated a hole several feet deep. The rock-and-gravel base under my logs was undermined and tumbled into this new abyss. Soon half, or even more, of the swollen streamflow would have poured under, rather than over, my dam. The first large uprooted tree rushing downstream, its mass of branches acting like a giant drogue in the current, was sure to hang up and rip out my logs as if they were matchsticks. I now saw clearly why most formal dams I'd seen on trout streams were completely planked with stout boards. They were necessary to help skid trees and boulders harmlessly over the top of the structure.

Reviewing my first season, I had to admit to a sorry record. First I had depleted my fishery through overharvesting. Then I had probably temporarily stunted it by stocking fish that might well depress future generations. And, for strike three, I had, like some latter-day King Canute, commanded the waters to do my bidding only to find that the river would have none of it.

However, the chagrin of failure began to fade as the winter slowly passed, and I started making new and better plans for the following season. And, as I did so, it dawned on me that I had become every bit as enthralled with the challenge of running a fishery as I ever had been by the sport of fly-fishing.

3

Fontinalis

Whenever I stepped into the West Branch with rod in hand, I couldn't shake off the feeling that I'd been transported back a century or more in time. A hundred years ago, all Catskill trout fishing—indeed, all trout fishing east of the Mississippi—was for brook trout exclusively. Pathetically few of these fisheries remain today. Pollution wiped out many of them. Warming turned others into brown-trout or smallmouth bass waters. Many were so ruthlessly overharvested that they now contain only put-and-take hatchery fish. The Neversink, because of altitude, sparse settlement, and long-standing private ownership barely escaped all three fates and remains one of the few viable wild-brook-trout rivers below the northernmost rim of New England.

The eastern brook trout, *Salvelinus fontinalis*, is a spectacular, almost gaudy fish. Its back and dorsal fin are dark green superimposed with a distinct, pale green, wormlike pattern. Its flanks are spotted with small red and blue dots and more plentiful, and larger, yellow ones. As an added fillip, the fins on the bottom of its body are red and edged with thin strips of contrasting black and white. It looks more like a fish you'd expect from the reefs off Tahiti than a native of our dour Northeast.

Though it pains me to admit this, the eastern brook trout, despite that official name, is technically not a true trout at all, but an extremely close relative called a char. The distinguishing differences are that chars have smaller scales and light spots on a darker background, while true trouts have dark spots on a light background. Fins, shape, and proportions are virtually identical. The brookie looks like a trout, swims like a trout, and tastes like a trout. Only a man with a degree in aquatic biology or the heart of a proctologist—or both—would think of calling it anything else.

Unfortunately, *Salvelinus fontinalis* is what the biologists term "extremely vulnerable to angling," which is just a postgraduate way of saying it can be as easy as hell to catch. Not every day or all day, perhaps, but when brookies are heavily on the feed their behavior ranges from not too discriminating to downright suicidal.

To make matters worse, the brookie is widely rated as the best-tasting of all the trouts. Don't be fooled by those white-fleshed synthetics sold frozen in supermarkets or served in fancy restaurants. They have all been raised in tanks and fed artificial food pellets—it's illegal to sell wild trout—and taste as much like wild brookies as Perdue fryers taste like native ruffed grouse.

This fatal combination of tastiness and gullibility led to the brook trout's near extinction on accessible reaches of the Neversink before the Civil War. Only after the state put restrictions on sizes and numbers and riparian owners exercised restraint did the fugitives from the headwaters repopulate the river's lower branches and a dozen or more miles of its main stem.

Another factor limiting wild brook trout populations is its demand for extremely pure and cold water. It's like a canary in a mine: When pollutants enter a stream, the brookie is the first fish to go belly up. It prefers water temperatures in the fifties, does well enough in the sixties, but either dies or moves into spring holes when temperatures rise into the seventies. Obviously this restricts its range, except in colder Canada, to cool streams or lakes and ponds with strong inflows of springwater. When the settlers cleared forests and dammed streams for waterpower, they destroyed countless miles of brook-trout habitat.

Yet it was this cold-water-loving characteristic that made the Neversink the Catskill's blue-ribbon trout river. Because it ran at a higher altitude and through shadier valleys, its waters were cooler than those of nearby rivers, and it was the largest brook-trout fishery in the region. The lower reaches of both the Beaver Kill and the Willowemoc were too warm for brookies, but even in midsummer the Neversink was cool enough for them for many miles below the junction of its two main branches at Claryville.

Any Neversink brook trout that stretches to nine inches or better has to be considered a good one, and this has probably always been true. Though I've nearly been misled by some thirteen- to fifteen-inch hatchery stockers, the largest brookie that I have ever seen taken from the river, and that I was certain was a native, measured twelve inches on the nose.

Two innate factors limit the size these fish can attain. The genetic strain native to this area is a slow-growing one. After a full year of river life, brookies average about four inches in length. At two years, most will measure seven inches. Any river fish nine inches or better is almost certainly a three-year-old.

It is also a short-lived fish. A trout's scales reveal the fish's age because annual growth rings on them show up under a microscope like rings on a tree stump. I have sent many scale samples from eleven-inch-plus monsters to experts at the Department of Environmental Conservation for age analysis, but none were pronounced to be over three years old. Some brookies in lower-stress Catskill ponds live four, rarely five, years and reach sixteen to seventeen inches, but individuals that have to fight currents all day, every day, seem to burn out before their fourth birthday.

Brook trout are essentially stay-at-home fish—at least the Neversink ones appear to be so. They are rarely caught in the reservoir so it can be presumed that they have little urge to migrate downstream as they grow larger. Concentrations of brookies near the mouths of spawning streams and spring-fed bogans also suggest that they spend most of their lives close to their birthplace. Further evidence: Brookies found well up in the branches of the river average about the same size as those in the main stem. The more mobile browns, on the other hand, are distinctly smaller upriver, indicating a downriver movement to bigger water as they grow larger.

Brook trout spawn in the fall, a few starting to "make the fish with two backs" as early as mid-October, and they're pretty well finished by early December. I've caught them in the act hundreds of times, and since they lose some caution when they have sex on their minds, I can get a close-up view if I move in slowly.

The paired male spends most of his time and energy chasing off smaller rivals and this is nearly a full-time job. The female does all the redd-digging, excavating gravel in flowing water or where a spring wells up by turning on her side and violently thrashing her tail. When she's created a depression several inches deep, she positions herself over the upcurrent end of this small pit and extrudes some of her eggs, triggering the attendant but nondigging male to release some of his milt. The eggs, now fertilized, sink to the bottom and are buried as soon as the female begins digging operations directly upcurrent for the next batch of eggs. Most brook trout are sexually mature by their second autumn of life, at about eighteen months, and it's not unusual to see five- and even four-inch fish doing grown-up work.

Brookies seldom compete for spawning space with the other salmonids later introduced into the river system because they rarely use sites on either the main-stem or lower sections of the two branches. They almost always head up the feeder streams when doing God's work, thus validating their name as "brook trout." They often use such tiny trickles that as my upstream neighbor, the retired fisheries biologist, puts it, "They'll spawn on wet leaves," and he's not exaggerating much. I've watched them dig redds in water so shallow that their dorsal fins and part of their backs were above the water surface.

Eggs overwinter under the gravel, hatching out in late March. However, they spend another few weeks under the sheltering gravel, living off the remnant yolk of their egg, which is suspended in a sac under their belly. This is provident of nature since it's a good bet that a snowmelt flood will occur about the first of April. Only when their yolk-food is used up do the fry wriggle up through the interstices of the gravel and begin stream life as dark, quivering commas, less than an inch long, tucked in behind stones and clumps of sedge in the brook margins.

A stream can accommodate only so many of these tens of thousands of fry. They must space themselves widely enough in the shallows so that they can't see one another. From the instant they emerge from the gravel, trout are fiercely territorial. This trait severely limits the number of fish that will find niches suitable for growth and safety.

By midsummer, when they've reached two inches in length, the thousands have been pruned to hundreds. Kingfishers, floodings, strandings, and other perils have weeded out all but the fittest or luckiest.

Fortunately, brook trout thrive in acidic, infertile waters far better than any other salmonid species. As long as their temperature requirements are met, they're not too demanding about depth, food supply, or overhead cover. Good-sized fish will often take up stations in smooth, fairly shallow stretches that no self-respecting brown trout would be caught dead in before dusk. This, however, may be more tolerance than preference on the Neversink, where the choicer lies are nearly always tenanted by big browns that will drive out smaller intruders.

The few uppermost miles of the West Branch, where it is only a large brook, is exclusively brook trout water. Browns start to appear as the stream gains depth and width, and they progressively increase in both numbers and size down to the confluence. The East Branch, which is less fertile and endowed with fewer deep pools, is for all practical purposes purely a brook-trout fishery right down to the junction.

The main-stem river is a fifty-fifty fishery. Brook trout still out-number the browns, but the average size of the latter is so much larger that the relative biomasses are about equal.

Today, however, just as it was in the beginning, the Neversink is not only the best major brook trout river in the Catskills, it is the only one. If you exclude their uppermost headwaters and small feeders, the other principal Catskill trout waters—the Beaver Kill, Willowemoc, Esopus, Schoharie, and both arms of the Delaware—are either brown trout or brown/rainbow fisheries.

I've referred to the Neversink strain of brookies a few times and perhaps that term needs explanation. Probably all the brook trout in the western Catskills had a common ancestral source: presumably a sea-run group that colonized the Delaware and its tributaries following the last Ice Age. However, warming water cut off access to the main stem of that river long ago, and the inhabitants of each major tributary have been isolated from each other for a few thousand years. Trout are genetically extremely plastic: Each environment ruthlessly selects, through Darwinian pruning, trout with traits necessary for survival in that particular river system. So it is nearly certain that Neversink fish now have innate characteristics that differ slightly even from those in the headwaters of the neighboring Willowemoc.

Brook trout are usually described as fish that rarely jump and prefer sunk flies to floaters. In my experience, this is true of most populations I've encountered in New England and Canada. Neversink brookies, on the other hand, take dry flies as readily as sunk ones, and on some evenings—especially in late May and in June—every decent one you hook will clear the water at least once.

As mentioned earlier, it is also the consensus that brookies are a cinch to catch when they're on the feed. But that is not necessarily so on this river. While they're not quite as picky as stream-bred brown trout, grown-up brookies will usually refuse, or only splash at, any fly that isn't a close imitation of the insect that's on their menu. This fastidiousness may be due to 150 years of culling the lesser intellects from the gene pool, but it is, nevertheless, a distinct Neversink characteristic.

A mixed fishery—one that holds more than one species of trout—has distinct advantages. One of these I've mentioned: Brook trout will often hold in water seldom used by the browns. This expands the area of fishable water on any stretch of river.

Also, brook trout will often feed at times of day when browns are inactive. This is especially true in midsummer. You can expect brookies to start rising an hour or more before browns come on the feed, which adds length to the viable fishing day as well.

I began to appreciate this bonus during a successful July evening that first summer. A thunderstorm the night before had raised shrunken water levels a few inches, restoring kick to the rapids and flow through the pools, and I had a hunch that this freshening might bring the fish on the feed well before the usual evening rise.

I set out as soon as the sun left the water at 6:00 P.M., a full hour before my usual starting time. I went to my furthest downstream pool and sat down near the tail end, waiting and watching. I couldn't make out any flies floating downcurrent, but I did see some smallish insects hovering up and down over the water. That was an encouraging sign and so was the sight of an occasional dimpling rise form sending a circle out over the smooth surface.

After marking a couple of risers nearly opposite me, I crept downstream thirty feet below them and eased into the river, babystepping very slowly so as not to send out warning ripples. When I reached a stand from which I could cover both of them handily, I pitched the large variant that was on my leader, a leftover from the morning's fishing, but it produced only one splashy refusal.

I reeled in, feeling that some research was in order. Bending forward, I scrutinized the square yard of water directly upstream of my boots. After a minute of staring, I spotted a small mayfly, dead, with wings spread flat in the surface film. I kept my eye on it as it slowly drifted below me, but once it was four feet past me it became invisible. No wonder I couldn't see what the fish had been taking. I went back to my vigil and when another fly, a duplicate of the first, appeared, I tried to pick it up and succeeded on the third try.

The fly had a reddish-brown body about one-third of an inch long and a pair of glassy half-inch wings. A No. 16 Red Quill Spinner seemed the nearest match in my box so I knotted one on and went back to work.

I cast this new offering a foot or more above one of the risers and the moment it hit the water it disappeared, but I knew within a few square inches where it had to be and focused on that spot. A few seconds later another dimple broke the surface and I raised my rod tip until I felt a solid throb. It was a brook trout better than nine inches long, and the deeply-cut mouth and reddish flanks—an early sign of the flamboyant spawning colors to come—told me it was a mature male fish. As I held it in my hand, admiring the tiny gemstones set in its flanks, I couldn't help thinking that my piously ascetic Vermont ancestors would have felt there had to be something sinful about a fish that dressed so ostentatiously. I decided he would also make sinfully delicious eating, and rapped him between the eyes with a small stone.

The commotion of playing and netting put the second fish down, but I stayed put until he recovered from his qualms and rose again. He, too, took on the very first cast, but since he was only eight inches, was granted a reprieve.

By now, rise forms were appearing more regularly and I inched up the pool, catching, or at least pricking, nearly every fish I cast to. By the time I'd worked up to the top of the pool I had landed ten trout and killed three. This stretch was now pretty well disturbed by my passage and a lot of its fish had sore mouths, so I took a shortcut through the bushes to the tail end of Home Pool, hoping to teach a few more trout that dieting is, indeed, good for the health.

In the next hour I caught another eight brookies on that same fly and lost several more. Apparently, I had picked out a winning imitation of the mayfly *plat du jour* and that pattern has become a top producer for me on midsummer evenings. But the real point of this parable is that I didn't touch or see a single brown trout until 8:30 P.M. Meanwhile, I had enjoyed a delicious two hours of brook trout fishing.

After all these years I am still startled by the rock-hard, going-away pull that follows the gentle sip of these relatively small fish. And that is the moment of exultation in fly-fishing—when you see the fish take your fly and feel the solid resistance as you pull the hook home. The tug-of-war that follows is pleasing, but it's not the sorcery that lures us back to the river again and again.

The intimacy and delicacy of this fishing lends it a unique charm. Even though a well-conditioned ten-incher will pull line off your reel and throw in a jump or two, such fish are rarely strong enough to break off.

And that's the sole drawback to brookie fishing: the utter predictability of their size limit. I have gone entire seasons without catching one over eleven inches. That's certainly a lovely, wild brook trout these days, but I couldn't call its capture either tackle-testing or heroic.

I had become resigned to this limitation until I read an article in the state's Department of Environmental Conservation magazine about two new "miracle" strains of brook trout that had been obtained from

Canada. These attained weights up to four or five pounds because they were fast growers with life spans of seven to eight years. These traits were presumably a special adaptation to the extremely short growing season up near the Arctic Circle.

The article said that populations had been built up in some private ponds in the Adirondacks under the supervision of fishery experts from Cornell University. The only drawback to this breakthrough was that the fish, like most wilderness brook trout, were so easy to catch that they might not last long enough to spawn in accessible waters, and so their stocking might have to be limited to remote walk-in ponds where fishing pressure was light.

The moment I put the magazine down I started a letter to the late Dwight Webster, a Cornell professor and the leading cold-water biologist of his day, outlining a proposal. Why not try these fish in a running-water environment as well? The Neversink, I pointed out, had ideal brook trout temperatures, and since nearly all of the upper river was in the hands of private owners who seldom killed fish, they would have every chance to survive and spawn.

I added that we needed only a few spawners or fertilized eggs to start such a program because we had several viable and flood-free ponds to raise fish for eventual release into the river. Halfway up the West Branch was a series of four ponds between a quarter acre and an acre in size, fed by a metered flow from a dam a quarter mile upriver that already contained a small population of wild brookies that had slipped in from the river. Each of the ponds was connected by short, rapid streams well-suited for spawning. I must have laid it on pretty thick because I soon received a return letter indicating interest and a strong probability that some fertile eggs might be available in early winter.

The two available subspecies had been appropriately named for the river systems where they had been discovered. The Assinicas were a chunky Canadian strain whose heaviness of body often disappeared in a new environment, and the Tamiscamies showed a distinctive patterning of extra-large, bright yellow spots. One biologist described them as looking like Christmas trees all lit up, and this arresting color pattern still showed up clearly after transplanting into Adirondack waters. Most important of all, these fish had been isolated from each other and from native fish by both physical and electric barriers to keep both sets of precious and desirable genes intact.

In late December I received about a thousand eyed, or fertile, Assinica eggs, and nearly froze my fingers solid by digging artificial redds in a fast-water section of stream between two of the ponds and then burying the eggs under loose, washed gravel. Apparently I was a good foster mother because next April the streamlet teemed with tiny fry. By early summer most were about two inches long and had dropped down into the five-foot-deep, half-acre pond below.

Word of these new "magic" fish soon spread up and down the Valley—especially among fishermen—and the pond received regular visitors. To cash in on this free labor pool we placed a large covered can of fish pellets beside the pond, and every sightseer seemed more than willing to chuck in a few handfuls to watch the fish boil. I doubt that any Strasbourg geese were ever better fed.

In the fall of their second full year, after two summers of lavish handouts, the Assinicas had grown into lovely, plump fish fifteen- to eighteen-inches long and weighing up to nearly three pounds. In September the male fish began to show bright red on their sides—the usual sign of sexual maturity. By late October, many were nosing up the small inlet stream looking for spawning territory, and when alarmed they raced back to the safety of the pond, throwing water like Chris-Crafts. I was sure we had it made. The next spring we could dip thousands of fry out of the streamlet to stock the river and the other three ponds.

It seems that it's when you're surest of success that you get blindsided. Near the bottom of this small spawning stream there had once been an outlet that led down to the river. Before I'd buried the eggs we had carefully blocked this off with chunks of sod faced with flat rocks. About the first of November, someone, perhaps out of malice or merely an unknowing child, had dug away this barrier. The fish must have sensed that bigger and better water lay in that direction, for all but a handful escaped down this channel during the following week.

The next summer, three of these outsized fish were recaptured from the river within a quarter mile of the pond. Where the rest of the two hundred or more ended up is still a mystery.

I wrote to the Adirondack hatchery, describing the near-success and great escape of the Assinicas, and asked for a refill. They replied that fingerlings might be available the following spring, but added that they'd had better success in establishing Tamiscamies in nearby ponds and offered those for our next try.

So we started all over again. The next spring I drove up to the Adirondacks in mid-April and brought back five hundred two-inch fingerlings that made the trip safely and were placed in the same pond. For some reason, this second attempt was not nearly as successful. The new fish didn't grow as rapidly, but perhaps that was because they lacked the celebrity of the first batch and got far fewer handouts. Then, too, the fish began to disappear, although we saw no dead bodies shining on the bottom of the pond. Perhaps the fish-eating mergansers or herons that usually stuck to the river had at last discovered this new deli.

The second summer, I took two dozen out of the pond and, after clipping their adipose fins so that they'd be instantly recognizable, put them in the nearby river. Most of these remained in place and grew a bit during the season, but none were recaptured the following year.

Interest in this stocking program fell off sharply and then virtually disappeared. There have been no "miracle" trout transplants in the past few years. Though they grew well in the ponds, perhaps Assinicas and

Tamiscamies, despite their intact, wild-trout genes, were somehow unsuited to life in the Neversink.

During the next few years I often lay in bed at night, wondering about those stockings. In my reveries, a small number of escapees survived, prospered, found each other at spawning time (trout pair off by size, when possible), and were creating new generations of a pure strain. So much of the river is lightly fished that this slowly increasing, discrete population might go undetected for quite a while. Of course this wishful thinking adds nothing to the fishery, but I can't imagine a lovelier way to drop off into sleep.

4

The Bad Old Days

The only style of fly-fishing that demands no intelligence or concentration is old-fashioned, downstream, sunk-fly fishing. You just knot on a likely or proven fly—perhaps even a team of two or three on short dropper-tippets—and inch your way down the center of a fast-water stretch, casting 45 degrees downcurrent, alternating right and left as you go.

The only thought process involved lies in choosing a well-populated riffle or run in the first place. For some reason, this simpleminded presentation rarely fools trout in the slow waters of flats and pools. On a small river you can cover every fish in the stretch this way, and it's surprising how high a percentage of them will snatch at the fly that's swinging past their noses.

Your sole duty is to stay somewhat awake, but there's not another blessed thing you need to do. With your fly traveling at the end of a tight, straight line, you couldn't possibly react in time to set the hook. By the time you feel the jolt of a take, the fish has either hooked itself or it hasn't. This is usually pleasant and productive fishing and its only drawback is that when you finally reel in, it's hard to convince yourself that you've managed to catch more fish than Boob McNutt would have if he'd been standing in your boots.

One Friday evening during my second summer I arrived upstate after an exhausting day at the office and decided that this lazy-man's fishing was all I was up to. I pulled on boots, took my rod off the pegs, and trudged down to the riffle at the very bottom of my water to cash in on the last half-hour before darkness.

I had rarely fished here before, having crossed it off as nursery water, and was surprised that three out of the seven brook trout I managed to land that night measured from eight to slightly better than nine inches. I'd passed my last posted sign and was reeling in when I saw a wader-clad figure emerge from the willows only twenty feet downstream. I waved and walked over to introduce myself.

The fisherperson turned out to be a lady in her middle years who identified herself as my downstream neighbor. Apparently relieved to learn that I wasn't a poacher after all, she invited me to fish her water, the uppermost section of the main-stem river, the following evening. Naturally I invited her to join me the next weekend on the water above, and this reciprocity soon became a frequent event.

In addition to being a skilled fly-fisher, she turned out to be the Valley's self-appointed historian as well. A few years earlier she had talked the local powers into letting her use a tiny room in the small town hall as a Valley museum. The museum's holdings consisted of several old maps, a few books on Catskill history, and a handful of artifacts and tools either donated or picked up at local garage sales.

The exhibit was open to the public on weekend afternoons but attracted such light traffic that I tried to drop in from time to time so she'd have someone to talk with during her often lonely hours as a volunteer. I was more than repaid for this small gesture since she told me much of what I know of Neversink Valley history and started me reading up on it.

While familiarizing myself with the exhibits I noticed what I thought was an obvious omission. I asked why there were no Indian artifacts—not even an arrowhead.

"I doubt that any have been found around here," she said. "At least I've never heard of any and don't expect to. Indians may have traveled through to reach the next valley, but they didn't hang around up here. They referred to the high Catskills as 'the dark forest' and that was probably a pretty apt description."

I was told that the Catskill landscape has been altered so drastically that an early-nineteenth-century traveler might not recognize it today. Originally, the Catskills were canopied with a stand of mature hemlocks three to four feet in diameter. Since hemlock is one of the few trees that can push up seedlings in dense shade, it was a self-perpetuating, or climax, forest. Whenever a mature tree died or blew down, a semidormant sapling shot up to exploit the vacated patch of sunlight.

This dark, year-round umbrella created a soft forest floor of discarded needles, bare except for the few hemlock seedlings. Grasses, forbs, berry bushes, and nut-bearing trees couldn't gain a foothold. There was virtually nothing for animals like deer, grouse, and turkey to eat. Except where floods, ice jams, or forest fires had cleared a place for food-bearing plants, this forest primeval offered little nourishment for man or beast. Only porcupines, squirrels, and the martens and fishers who preyed on them, could scratch out a living.

During the late eighteenth and early nineteenth centuries, venturesome outdoorsmen from the lowlands explored the area on horseback or hiked in from the nearest stagecoach stop and found the Neversink teeming with small, dark brook trout. These early anglers camped out, ate all the trout they could hold, and lugged out as many as they could carry—even though most of their catch was sure to putrefy on the long trip home. Except for these brief incursions, the Catskills were little trafficked.

It took the hemlocks to draw the first year-round settlers. Back in those days, the liquid obtained from boiling hemlock bark was the standard tanning agent, and since it took several tons of bark chips to cure a ton of hides, it made economic sense to cart the raw skins to where the hemlocks stood. Tanneries sprang up in the eastern Catskills near the Hudson waterway during the early nineteenth century, and when the Erie Railroad laid track up the Delaware Valley, the western part of the mountains were opened up, too. Tanneries leapfrogged one another up into the higher valleys and the upper Neversink Valley was no exception. In 1847 a tannery was set up in what is now Claryville and the scalping of the neighboring hills began.

The coming of the Civil War created a huge boom for the tanneries and they expanded operations as quickly as they could. The Union Army needed saddles, harnesses, belts, cartridge cases, and lots of them, in a hurry. Shiploads of South American hides were rushed to the seemingly endless stands of Catskill hemlocks.

Boarding facilities were erected to house the expanding logging and tannery crews, and the hamlet of Claryville took shape. Except for two white clapboard houses where the managers once lived, only two other vestiges of this frenetic activity remain. One is the old tannery chimney that still pokes up, undamaged, at the southern edge of town. The other is a distinct, undulating pattern that looks like giant corduroy and is found on the forest floors of some of the higher, surrounding hills. This is the humus remnant of the huge, virgin tree trunks that were stripped of their bark and left to rot where they lay. Only the more accessible logs ever made it to the overloaded sawmills.

As the loggers moved farther up the Valley, settlers from lower down moved in behind them, homesteading the clear-cut hillsides. For a few years they eked out a living by cutting the grass that had sprung up and selling hay to the loggers as fodder for the oxen that hauled sleds and carts of peeled bark down the slopes.

When the loggers finally moved on, the short boom was over. The flat valley floor around Claryville was just viable for farming, and that part of the settlement remains to this day. The hillside hayers tried to hang on by subsistence farming, but couldn't make a go of it. The poor, thin, acidic soil and short growing season doomed them. Today, only the jumbled rocks of old cellar holes and a few ancient apple trees mark the sites of these failed upland farms.

Their stump-and-grass fields were quickly colonized by hardwoods: beech, black cherry, yellow birch, ash, oak, and maple. An ancient resident once told me that when she was a girl back at the turn of the century, there wasn't a stick of timber on the surrounding hills thicker than two or three inches in diameter.

In the nearby Beaverkill and Delaware valleys, these "pole trees" were harvested in their infancy. For several decades they were sawed into four-foot lengths and hauled off as fodder for the new acid factories that had replaced the tanneries. Their small trunks were converted into charcoal, and the fumes given off during this process were distilled into wood alcohol and acetone—a key ingredient in making the celluloid collars that were de rigueur in those days.

Fortunately, the Neversink Valley escaped this second deforestation. Perhaps demand for charcoal and celluloid wasn't brisk enough to warrant operations in high, remote valleys. No acid factory was installed at Claryville, and the surrounding hardwood forests with their sprinkling of conifers have enjoyed 120 years of relatively undisturbed growth.

But that first denuding of the mountains changed the Neversink River, perhaps forever. Once the dense protective canopy had been reduced to bare fields, runoff from even a modest rain turned violent and muddy. Spring floods increased in ferocity, too. Without the evergreen overstory, the sun in late March and early April poured through the bare hardwood branches causing unnaturally sudden snowmelt. Small seasonal torrents stripped the steep slopes of what little humus or topsoil they had managed to accumulate over the years and the resulting floods ripped out retaining, bank-side trees, rootballs and all. Adding to this destruction, farmers foolishly clear-cut trees right down to the river's edge to enlarge their meager hayfields.

In a few short years the river had been altered beyond recognition. The once fairly stable waterway now went up and down like a yo-yo. Even as the hills began to heal themselves with volunteer seedlings, rampaging floods continued to vandalize the riverbed. With the loss of bordering trees that had anchored banks and channeled flows, the river widened, shallowed, and even braided in places. Freed gravel and cobbles tumbled downstream. Pools filled in. Deep runs turned into wide, shallow riffles.

At the opposite end of the scale, summer flows shrank to previously unheard-of lows. During their growing season the new hardwoods, which require several times as much water as evergreens do, sucked up moisture that had previously fed the river. Summer flow was often reduced to little more than a trickle.

The increasing number of sawmills that had sprung up to harvest the white pines that grew in the valley floor not only gouged the streambed while running logs down to their saws, but also flushed bark and sawdust into the river, using it as a handy sewer. This destructive practice continued even after the turn of the century. In the early 1900s, Theodore Gordon wrote, "How we detest a sawmill on one of our favorite streams! The sappy, heavy sawdust not only floats on the surface, but sinks to the bottom and permeates the entire river. The trout will not rise . . ." Very likely there was another reason why trout wouldn't rise in so abused a stream: Most of them had been killed off.

Along with the polluting, widening, and shallowing of the river, its waters had warmed up, too. With the shading canopy of evergreens gone, the sun beat down on the cleared hillsides, drying up springs that had chilled the river. As summer water temperature climbed, the trout retreated upstream.

As if the degradation of the environment wasn't deadly enough, men tried to exterminate the surviving fish. Hungry loggers and farmers resorted to nets, spears, poisons, and dynamite as well as hook and line to fill their frying pans. Even "sportsmen" from the city played a part in this near-annihilation. There are documented records of single anglers killing several hundred trout during a weekend outing.

It didn't take long for such practices to create a trout-fishing wasteland. Even before the Civil War made its pressing demands on the hemlocks, most of the Catskills had been written off by anglers. An article in the July, 1859, issue of *Harper's New Monthly Magazine* fulsomely lamented, "The banks of the Beaverkill and the Willerwhemack (sic), tributaries of the Delaware, twenty years ago were famous for brook trout, and were once favorite places for the lovers of piscatorial sports. These haunts, where genius once found leisure from the toils of city life, with thousands of others which a few years ago abounded in game, are now deserted, and fret their way on to the ocean, stained by tan and thickened by the refuse wood that tumbles from the teeth of the grating saw." Undoubtedly, the Neversink was in no better shape.

Conditions hadn't improved much a decade after the war. An 1874 article in *Forest and Stream* reported, "The Beaverkill and the Neversink rivers, the most important streams in this region, have for many years been well known to New York sportsmen, and are now almost abandoned, and considered 'fished out'."

With the tree bark gone and farming a bust, the trout, though thinned to pathetic numbers, took center stage again. It may seem improbable that a small animal, standing on a low rung of the vertebrate ladder and possessing no commercial value, could exert so much influence. Yet the trout, more than any other single factor, revived and even shaped the entire upper Valley.

Sportfishing, which had long been a privilege of the British upper classes, spread across the Atlantic and was adopted by the new class of monied Americans created after the Civil War. Inns and boarding houses catering to city sportsmen began to spring up on the choicer Catskill rivers as early as the 1870s.

One of these, known as the Parker Place, was situated on a small flat four miles up the West Branch of the Neversink. Martin Parker, realizing that a depleted fishery was no great attraction, was one of the first to stock his stretch of stream to lure angler-guests. He also posted and patrolled it in an attempt to keep some of his trout in the water long enough for his city sportsmen to get a crack at them.

Posting and patrolling, both widespread today, enraged local anglers back in the 1870s. They poached Parker's waters with renewed intensity, abusing his stream guardians and doing everything in their power to make life miserable for his paying guests. Parker fought it out for a few years, but it was a losing battle. In 1882 he sold out to one of his frequent guests and never returned.

The new owner, a wealthy New Yorker named Clarence Roof, was made of sterner stuff and had deeper pockets. He arrested trespassers and hauled them into court. For the next several years "The Great Trout Wars," as a local paper named them, were waged over Roof's water.

He spared neither effort nor expense. He rerouted the Valley road several hundred yards up the hillside, where passersby wouldn't be tempted to stop and fish. He imported high-powered lawyers from New York City to prosecute those caught red-handed.

One of these, Ralph Govin, spent so much time on legal cases in the Valley that he fell in love with the area. He picked up a string of failed farms on the East Branch, piecing together five miles of Valley floor and gaining riparian rights from the junction on up. Roof, meanwhile, kept adding to the Parker holdings until he, too, owned five uninterrupted miles on the other branch—and this is the holding the Queen of the West Branch inherited. By the turn of the century, major dynasties were established up both branches.

Gradually, Roof began to gain the upper hand. Convictions, some with heavy fines, played a part. Perhaps his most telling weapon was a stern policy of never hiring or buying anything from the family of anyone caught poaching. In a valley where he was the major employer, this threat had teeth in it.

Govin was nearly as successful with a more subtle approach. He hired the most flagrant poacher in town as his head patroller. The message of the sanctity of riparian rights began to sink in and soon became so indelible that, even today, poaching by the descendants of the Valley's old trout-warriors is rare indeed.

Edward Ringwood Hewitt started putting together his "princely" five miles on the main-stem river in 1917. For several decades until his death in the 1950s, he was far and away America's most famous angler. Born to a wealthy New York City family, he fished the finest trout and salmon waters of North America and Europe—often in the company of the great or near-great.

Hewitt was far more than a rich, self-indulgent fishing bum, though. He was also a prolific author, engineer, inventor, and sometime industrialist. He held strong opinions on nearly every known subject and expressed them so unflinchingly that opponents claimed he was "always positive and sometimes right."

The fishery he ran on the Neversink was a first-class one all the way. He designed and built a series of expensive planked dams to create better habitat for his trout. He installed and supervised his own private fish hatchery, raising outsized fish to release into his stretch of river. Then, to keep them in top condition and happily in place, he had them fed a rich meat diet at regular intervals.

Each September he and his fishing guests set about catching as many of his aquatic protégés as possible, stockpiling them for next season in specially constructed spring-fed ponds. When some of his fish played truant despite his coddling, they were sternly brought back to Hewitt's water.

The Queen of the West Branch, who had been an intimate friend of his, told me that nearly every year Hewitt would drive up to her house in his Packard touring car with a huge tub in the back seat and announce, "Some of my big fish have strayed up into your water and I've come to fetch them back." The Queen's son, who often accompanied Hewitt on these missions, says Hewitt was such a magician with the fly rod that he could, indeed, catch nearly all the big fish he could spot in a pool.

One of the major disappointments in my life is that I never met nor fished with Ed Hewitt. He died, well into his nineties, several years before I entered the Valley.

During the twenties and thirties, most of the water between Hewitt and the junction was purchased by weekenders from the city. While posting and patrolling may have been lackadaisical on some of these beats until fairly recently, the upper Neversink has been an essentially private fishery since World War II, and most of it had been closed off well before then.

Year-round residents seem to have forgotten their great-grandparents' resentment of Roof and other river-posting landowners, and their relations with summer people are nearly friction-free. Lifestyles of the weekenders are simple when they're up-country—there's little entertaining and no ostentation. There are no Rolls-Royces in the Valley and not even a BMW or a Mercedes.

Still, there's probably an undercurrent of feeling toward those who depart for warmer parts each fall and leave the shivering to the natives. One man, who chucked a city job for year-round residency, now raises a small herd of pricey breeding cattle, has become a pillar of the Volunteer Fire Department, and blends in with the local population.

I once asked him what he thought of the Valley's newest summer weekender, adding, "I think he's a hell of a nice guy and an asset to the Valley, don't you?"

"He seems like your typical bright-lighter to me."

"What does that mean?"

"Oh, he thinks he's doing me a favor taking free manure off my hands."

"I meant, what the hell's a bright-lighter?"

"You know, a fellow who comes up from the big city on weekends."

"So that's what the apple-knockers call us."

"What the hell's an apple-knocker?"

There are still a few handymen, carpenters, and plumbers working out of the Valley, but except for a small, family-staffed convenience store, there are no businesses and no steady employment. The general store and two-man sawmill both failed several years ago. Since the township of Neversink, of which Claryville is part, has voted dry for years, there are no resort hotels in the Valley.

Farming has been reduced to a little haying and small kitchen gardens. Two or three residents raise a few head of livestock, but most don't even bother with backyard chickens anymore. Employed natives get in their cars and drive to jobs in neighboring valleys. It is said that there are fewer year-round residents in the upper Valley than there were at the turn of the century, and I have every reason to believe this is true.

5

"Let us now praise . . ."

If I could claim that our year-round residents shared distinctive personality traits it would certainly lend color and charm to the Neversink Valley. The prototypical Vermonter, Chesapeake Bay waterman, and southwestern cowboy clearly enrich the folklore of those areas. However, I can't detect, and refuse to create, any indigenous Neverkill characteristics. The natives here seem to me to be much like rural people in other regions who have, in the last generation or two, given up small farming for wage-earning.

The same is true of the "bright-lighters." The only common denominator they seem to share is that most, but not all, enjoy trout fishing. This commonality of interest acts as a governor on social activity. During most of the season the best fishing occurs at dusk, and no fly-fisher with any say in the matter would squander Saturday evening by showering, putting on tie and jacket, and getting tiddly at a cocktail party. Seashore weekenders seem to kick the gong around at a frenetic pace, but those who escape to the mountains appear to be looking for solitude. The little entertaining that takes place usually occurs at midday when fishing's at its worst—and that's a poor time of day for a bacchanalia or an orgy.

And yet, despite its low-key atmosphere, the Valley has played host to a number of prominent and interesting people. Again, it was usually the fishing that attracted them.

Perhaps the first of these was the naturalist John Burroughs. As a young man, he slipped into the Valley from his home in Roxbury to the north, and described the river as being paved with small trout.

Years later, he was a frequent houseguest at Roof's place on the West Branch, and in his later days he spent two years there being nursed back to health on a rice diet by the Queen, who had inherited the estate. She told me he was a keen angler, although his approach was more practical than puristic. When the fish weren't biting well, he'd snip the feathers off his fly hook and furtively impale a stick-caddis grub on it until he'd filled his creel.

The next giant to enter the Valley was a *nouveau-pauvre* gentleman named Theodore Gordon. Born into a wealthy southern family, Gordon was pauperized in early adulthood when the family interest in a railroad company was wiped out by a shady manipulation. From the mid-1880s until his death in 1915, he lived in the Catskills, mainly on the Neversink, eking out a marginal existence by writing short pieces for outdoor magazines and selling his hand-tied flies to visiting sports.

The few surviving photos portray Gordon as a short, scrawny man with a dense black mustache. He usually waded the river wet— that is, without boots or waders—and this practice played merry hell with the circulation in his legs as the years went on. It is believed that he also suffered from tuberculosis and that this, perhaps coupled with a bout of pneumonia, killed him while he was still in his fifties.

The impoverished Gordon could never afford a house, and either boarded with a local family or lived in a furnished room near the river. He never owned any water either, but that was no privation because the entire main-stem river below the Roof and Govin holdings was unposted in his day. Indeed, as he pointed out in several of his published pieces, he preferred public to private fisheries, complaining that the latter were usually overstocked and so easy that he learned nothing from fishing them.

In 1890, Gordon wrote a letter to the great Frederic M. Halford in England, who had recently authored the first book describing trout fishing with a floating fly. He soon received a gracious reply with samples of Halford's patterns hooked into the margins. Gordon began adapting those examples to insects he found on the Neversink, and thereby launched dry-fly fishing in America.

He is best remembered today for the popular fly pattern that bears his name, the Quill Gordon. This fly is still considered the best imitation of a sooty, early-season mayfly named *Epeorus pluralis,* but I'm convinced that Gordon never intended this matchup. I have seen examples of these Quills as he tied them and they differ widely from today's dark dun-hackled dressings. He used pale, silvery hackle and wrote that he dyed the black-and-white peacock quill bodies to various shades of yellow as the season advanced. It seems likely that these flies were intended to be imitations of the June mayfly we now call the Light Cahill.

In recent years, Gordon has become a cult figure. He did, indeed, write about fly-fishing with a graceful, near-angelic style, but the man himself was probably bitter, broken, and irascible. Years ago I discussed Gordon with men who had fished with him and bought flies from him in their youth. They told me he was secretive (he never let anyone watch him tie flies) and often ill-tempered toward fellow anglers— especially bait-fishers. I find these charges entirely believable. (One of the biggest turds I have ever known wrote prose that sounded as if it issued from a seraph.) But Gordon's enormous contributions to, and writings on, trout fishing shouldn't be diminished by any real or imagined quirks of his personality.

Hewitt was the Valley's next towering figure and I've covered him once-over-lightly in the previous chapter. Fly patterns he developed on his water, such as the Bivisible and Neversink Skater series, were coast-to-coast favorites for decades. In his later years, he rented out rod privileges on his five miles to fishing friends, many of whom were nearly as famous as he was. Weekends on his water must have seemed like the fly-fishing version of an All-Star game.

George M. L. LaBranche was a frequent fishing companion who, along with Hewitt and Ambrose Monell, pioneered the technique of fishing the dry fly for Atlantic salmon on Canadian rivers. LaBranche's seminal 1914 book, *The Dry Fly and Fast Water*, describing his method of prospecting for and enticing trout that were not rising or visibly feeding, converted an entire generation of fly-fishers. He was an elegant Wall Streeter who was always impeccably attired when on the stream. I have watched home-movie clips of him fishing the Neversink and he was easily the most stylish caster I have ever seen.

John Alden Knight, who was nearly as famous as LaBranche during the Hewitt era, was a regular invitee. His books and articles on fly-fishing and wing shooting were taken as gospel during the 1920s and 1930s. His writings stand up well even today, but I feel his authority is tarnished by his publication of the annual Solunar Tables. These were schedules of the best fishing hours for every day in the coming year, predicted by the moon's pull on the tides. Such a force may, indeed, influence feeding patterns on oceanic fish, but to claim they also affect fish behavior in running fresh water borders is, I feel, on the fraudulent.

Since these celebrity outings took place well before my residence in the Valley, I never met either LaBranche or Knight, but I did know the late dean of American fly-fishing writers, Sparse Grey Hackle, who was also one of the "Neversink Rods," as Hewitt called them. Sparse was a tireless raconteur and a walking memory bank of arcane fishing facts and historic happenings. Those who frequently fished with him have told me that Sparse's oratorical leanings were so overpowering that they severely restricted his fishing—at least during his last twenty years. After they'd arrived at the river, pulled on waders, and set up rods, Sparse could be counted on to sit down on the riverbank and start reminiscing out loud. No matter how many fish could be seen rising out on the river, no one dared to sneak away with rod in hand while this commanding figure was holding forth.

Herbert Hoover almost, but not quite, fished the Neversink. The Queen of the West Branch, who was one of his great admirers, frequently invited him to be her guest in the years following his incumbency. He usually accepted this invitation, but at the last moment always got involved in some project that made a visit impossible. The Queen once showed me Hoover's letters. They were warm, witty, and enormously human—quite unlike the stern face that appears above the celluloid collar in stock photos.

One of the Valley's most observant and innovative flytiers has somehow slipped through the pages of angling history. Ed Sens, who owned a stretch of the main stem during the 1930s and 1940s, created realistic patterns imitating emerging caddis pupae decades before anyone else paid any attention to caddisflies in any of their life-stages. Surprisingly, no present Valley resident remembers him well, although one thought he'd been an engineering executive in a large, famous corporation. Sens left us no book, but his frequent fishing companion, Ray Ovington, wrote about the effectiveness of Sens's fly patterns in *How to Take Trout on Wet Flies and Nymphs.*

No account of the region would be complete without mentioning the other queen in the Valley—the one who ruled over the East Branch. She had inherited Ralph Govin's water, and even though her stretch dwindled over the years from five miles to a measly two, she easily ranked as royalty. She wasn't in residence during my first season in the Valley, and when I asked a neighbor about her, he said, "Just wait till you meet her . . . she's the sexiest-looking sixty-year-old woman you'll ever see."

Since I was then in my early thirties, I couldn't believe my ears. A sexy-looking sixty-year-old woman? I suspected the man was some sort of necrophiliac or perhaps a closet taxidermist.

When I finally met her the following year I felt like amputating my tongue. She was built like a racing sloop, had bright yellow (honest) hair, and the most electric-blue eyes I've ever looked into. She was an accomplished horsewoman and avid fly-fisher. Whenever I'd drop by and suggest we go fishing, she'd leap up, hurry into her waders, and always beat me into the river.

I was clearly smitten, but even my nonfishing and potentially jealous wife adored her. Never before or since have I felt such acute anguish over having been born thirty years too late.

With such a matriarchal hierarchy in the Valley, wasn't there a queen of the main stem as well? After the death of Hewitt, who was clearly the king of the big river, there were two princesses to choose from. However, remembering the fracas Paris started by judging women, I'll have to leave that title open. Since the queens of both branches are now dead, the issue seems academic anyway.

6

Trutta

Near the end of my third summer in the Valley I learned that one of the Queen's daughters and her family had moved back into New York City from out of state, and knew that meant the end of my tenancy. This was a disappointment but not a catastrophe. Fortunately, I had—if not an ace—at least a face card up my sleeve.

The year before, an acquaintance from a trout club downriver had offered me a piece of river land that he owned but had never built on. He was retiring, planned to summer in Canada and winter in the Bahamas, and felt no need for property within striking distance of New York City. The price he asked—little more than he'd paid years before—seemed so reasonable that I considered it a wise long-term investment even though, at the time, I had no intention of moving down there.

The property was a pie-shaped piece of about twenty-five acres and included a half mile of the main-stem river and a splendid, level building site overlooking the river from an elevation of thirty feet. While we planned and built a small lodge on this spot, we rented a hillside cabin up the East Branch as a temporary foothold in the Valley, and I began fishing my new water, five miles below, from this base.

The top end of this fishery began about two hundred feet above the house site and was only a wide, unproductive riffle running diagonally from the left, toward the house, through a hundred-yard-wide floodplain of cobbles and small willow clumps. Its flat, eroded expanse gave evidence that the river channel in this section was extremely fickle and had changed course back and forth through the area frequently and recently, since there were no mature, or even young, hardwoods or evergreens in the entire area. In fact, much of this rubble bed was covered with water every time the river rose a mere two feet.

Where the riffle hit the riverbank just below the building site, it had dug a good pool with a few large boulders that had been tumbled off the steep hillside at the head of it. After about forty feet, this slow-water stretch shallowed out into more of a flat, about two-and-a-half-feet deep. The better fish bunched up in the deep top end, but there were fair-sized brook trout all the way down to the tail end where the water quickened into another rapids.

After a brief run, the flow slammed into a steep hillside which abruptly pushed the river nearly 90 degrees to the left, so that it then ran due south. I expected to find a deep, spectacular pool with a strong eddy in such a place, but that was not to be the case here. The land contours dropped away so rapidly in this section that there were three deep, steplike pockets instead. Since these hold excellent fish, the net gain to the fishery is about the same as if one good pool had, indeed, been formed there.

When the riverbed flattened out again below, there was a seventy-five-foot-long pool with the main thread running down the right side, only a few feet away from a vertical rock cliff. The top half of the pool was four- to five-feet deep and held an occasional very large fish. There were productive lies all the way down to the tail end, though, because the rock seam at the base of the cliff had been deeply undercut, creating an underwater cavern that extended nearly the full length of the pool and provided the fish with ideal overhead cover and easy lies out of the stronger, nearby current. This lovely spot virtually named itself: "Cliff Pool."

At the tail end a series of large rocks lay stepped across the river, which both slowed and raised the water in the pool above. More importantly, they were arranged diagonally, at a 45-degree angle to the flow, so they shunted the main current back toward the cliffs again, creating a deep hole where it ricocheted off the rock face. This I named "Cliff Pocket."

Below this ran another hundred yards of medium-paced riffle that was featureless and usually fishless until the water slowed again into a 150-foot-long flat. Although it was only about three feet deep at low water, it usually held several good fish because it contained some large boulders and undercut rock slabs for cover. This stretch remained nameless until I improved it a few years later.

The flat ended in a short riffle, which pitched into another stretch of slow water below. The riverbed widened here, producing a shallow, unproductive center section, but there were deeper current-threads along each bank with enough cover to be interesting. At the tail end, a diagonal bar of rubble threw the flow over to the steep right bank again, creating a slow run studded with big rocks. Below this, the water belonged to my downstream neighbor.

My new water was shaped much like a boomerang with the upper arm slightly shorter than the lower one. Most of the best fishing lay in the lower two-thirds, where the river ran along a steep hill on the right and was contained on the left by a six-foot-high bank securely anchored with mature trees.

With over twice the volume of flow, this section of river was not only wider and deeper than the West Branch water, it also held more pools and flats because of its gentler gradient and averaged a couple of degrees warmer. The combination of these characteristics exerted a distinct influence on the resident fish populations. While the smaller, faster water I'd just left had produced mostly brook trout—there were only three or four places where you could expect a decent brown to hold—my new water was trying to become a brown-trout fishery. Though these fish were usually harder to fool than the brookies, the knowledge that my very next cast might raise a trout of from three-quarters of a pound up to two or more added a new dimension of excitement to the fishing.

On some evenings—usually when a low or falling barometer depresses conditions—I catch only brook trout. Browns simply won't rise (or at least I can't raise any), which indicates they're especially sensitive to weather conditions. Harder to explain are the very few times when every fish I take is a brown and I could swear there wasn't a brookie in the river. Most often, though, I end up catching both species, but at different times and in different places.

This separation of species by habit and habitat is most noticeable at dusk. During my first season on the big water I noted this phenomenon, and the August 5 entry in my fishing diary records the resultant change in my evening fishing tactics.

> "Day cloudy, low 60s, thunderstorm at 5:00, blue skies by 6:00. Went to lower water at 7:00. Water 63. Almost no flies. 7 brookies from bottom halves of flat and Cliff—#16 Red Spinner. Changed to G.F.V., looped back and fished up throats of both. 3 browns, 9, 12½, 14½. Flashlight!"

My spastic code language brings back that evening to me, but probably needs some translating if anyone else is to understand it. A storm system passed through in late afternoon and was followed by clearing and a rising barometer, which is good for fishing. The walk downriver takes nearly a quarter of an hour, so I started actual fishing at 7:15 P.M. Right away I noticed a few risers in the bottom half of the flat, pussyfooted below them, and took four brookies—two of them good ones—with the tactics I described in the earlier chapter on brook trout. Then I detoured through the woods up to the tail of Cliff Pool and took three more, being careful in both places not to go near, and possibly disturb, the faster water up near their heads.

With only a half hour of daylight left, I changed to a bushy Grey Fox Variant and circled back down to the top end of the flat. After five minutes of watching and no decent rises seen, I decided to go prospecting. I started with the streamy water, working up to the choppy water of the inlet run. That didn't take long to cover because if there's a good brown out looking for a meal, he'll nearly always be in the dead center of the current-thread. This line was clearly defined by a bubble-path, and by lengthening each cast by a foot or so I was exploring the water at a steady pace. When my fly landed in the beginning of the chop, I saw a boil and struck a solid fish. This was the twelve-and-a-half incher and he ran upstream and jumped before I could lead him down and play him out.

His upcurrent charge had certainly spooked any fish that might have been lying above him, so I took my business up to Cliff Pool again, fishing its throat in exactly the same manner. A fish rose in the fast slick soon after I'd started, boring away strongly, but when it finally jumped I could see it was only a feisty nine-incher.

I was tempted to head back to the house when I saw the first bat of the evening, but decided instead to fish out the rest of the stretch. I was casting my fly, which I could no longer see, well up into the choppy water when I saw a small flash of white and pulled back into something that felt like a snag.

I finally got that fish in, but by then it was too dark to read the scale on my rod, so the fourteen-and-a-half-inch length is only a guesstimate. Finding my way back through the pitch-black woods and crossing the river in front of my house was finally accomplished— partly by groping and partly by stargazing—and I had two long, red scratches on my face to remind me to slip a small flashlight into my fishing vest.

As you probably know, the brown trout, *Salmo trutta*, is not a native species but a relatively recent transplant from across the Atlantic. The first shipment of eyed, or fertile, eggs didn't reach our shores until 1883. These were a gift sent from a German fish culturist to Fred Mather, a New York State hatcheryman. The next year Mather started receiving eggs from British fish as well, and these two slightly different strains were soon thoroughly mixed. The genes of both coexist in the fish we catch today.

In 1886, a group of sportsmen stocked browns in Aden Brook—a medium-sized tributary that now empties into the midsection of the reservoir—making the Neversink system one of the first in America to receive this new species. The fish survived, spawned, and their descendents quickly colonized a large section of the river both above and below Aden Brook. Very large trout were soon being caught—or, more often, hooked and broken off. How big is "very large"? Since Theodore Gordon wrote that he'd never seen a brook trout over fourteen inches taken from any Catskill stream, a man could probably dine out on stories of any capture that bettered the pound mark.

Despite this greater size potential, browns were, at first, widely denounced as "cannibals" that were eating up the local brookies. This was probably unfair. Warming of the water from logging and settlement, along with increased sewage and effluent from small factories, were enough to do in, or drive out, the brook trout without any help from the browns. These hardier, more tolerant fish simply took over vacated territory.

Browns were also bad-mouthed for a far more valid reason: The average angler couldn't catch them. Standard terminal tackle in the brook-trout era was a team of three gaudy wet flies whipped onto heavy gut snells. When this rig was dragged through the water, it took in a lot of naive brookies, but very few of the more sophisticated browns.

These European trout had been selectively pruned for centuries. Those that were easy to gull had been quickly yanked out and removed from the gene pool, while the more discriminating survived and spawned. This is in no way a claim that the descendents became intellectuals, but the process did produce a fish with the congenital habit of suspiciously scrutinizing any object before taking it into its mouth. Gordon and a few of his friends, who adopted the British technique of presenting a single, small, insect-imitating fly on a fine, tapered leader, were brown trout enthusiasts from the start.

As recently as the 1920s and 1930s, many anglers still called browns "Germans"—using the word with the pejorative connotations whipped up by propagandists during World War I. It wasn't until after the Second World War that this species became widely admired.

Today, it is the standard all-American trout. Except in a small brook-trout enclave in northern New England, and amongst a few rainbow and cutthroat diehards in the Pacific Northwest, the word "trout" today means brown trout. In fact, most of our famous fisheries owe their reputations to this hardy species. This is certainly true of the lower Willowemoc and main-stem Beaver Kill, neither of which were rated as trout fisheries until this higher-temperature-tolerant species was introduced.

The colder, less fertile Neversink embraced this new trout only halfheartedly. Though their growth-rate and spawning success seem adequate, brown trout populations in the Neversink never exploded as they did on other nearby waters. Without the brook trout supplement, fishing in the Neversink today would be a thin proposition.

Although their appearance varies widely with environment, brown trout are easy to identify. Only silvery, sea-run specimens, which are sometimes mistaken for Atlantic salmon grilse, are likely to be misidentified. Browns have fewer and far larger spots (with a scattering of rust-brown ones, in most cases) than rainbows, and an orange or orange-spotted adipose fin just ahead of their tails. You could never mistake one for the greenish brook trout.

Neversink browns closely resemble their relatives in other Catskill streams except that they're usually a bit more streamlined. All browns slightly change both shape and color as they grow older. Small, immature fish tend to be slim and silvery. In the prime of young adulthood, their sides and bellies turn a lovely butter color and their shapes fill out some. As they approach senility, however, they tend toward rusty brown, their tail fins become convex, and their caudal peduncles—the wrists just ahead of their tails—look swollen and gross.

Browns in the Neversink grow faster than brookies do. In their second summer, at the age of one-year-plus, they average six inches long. The following season they'll measure nine or ten inches, and by their third year, when they've reached sexual maturity, they've grown to a foot or more.

They also live longer than brookies. It is said that brown trout have a life expectancy of up to thirteen years, but that span is probably never attained in fast-water environments. I have fished corpses off the stream bottom that showed no signs of injury or disease, and had apparently died of old age, whose scales revealed they were only seven years old.

As mentioned earlier, mature browns dominate the choicest feed lanes and lies. They have a strong attachment for overhead cover as well and only in the deepest pools will you find a good fish far from a sunken log, undercut rock slab, cutbank, or root snag.

This is one manifestation of their aversion to bright, sunny conditions. Another is that during the summer they rarely take up feeding stations in the open until just before dark, as I pointed out earlier. In their final days they are said to become mainly nocturnal. Even in their prime they are distinctly crepuscular.

Browns are reputed to take floating flies—both natural and artificial—more readily than other trouts, but I'm not sure this is an inborn characteristic. They tend to thrive in warmer, more fertile streams that produce larger insect hatches, and the high volume of surface food in such environments may be responsible for this reputation. At any rate, Neversink browns don't seem to rise more readily than the brookies do, and even when they do, they seem to do so for a shorter time period.

Especially in their prime years, browns jump regularly when hooked. They may not be as acrobatic as rainbows, but they'll outleap most brookies. You can expect two or three water-clearing jumps from a good Neversink brownie before he gives up. The rusty old-stagers, though, usually stick to a submerged game of tug-of-war.

While an occasional brown may occupy the same choice lie for years, most are wanderers, always on the lookout for better quarters in their immediate area. Remove a good brown from a protected lie and within a day or two another of nearly the same size will take it over. As winter approaches, browns will drift downstream, searching for deep, slow water. Conversely, when temperatures rise toward lukewarm in summer, they'll push up into the cooler flows near the headwaters.

Most also migrate upriver just prior to spawning in October. Before the reservoir dam cut off access from the lower river, a run of large browns into the upper section was a regular August feature. Even today we expect a run of large reservoir fish at that time of year after each good spate, but this is usually a limited bonus since the reservoir trout population is surprisingly sparse.

Their spawning ritual is almost identical to the brook trouts' and takes place at nearly the same time. However, browns choose different sites. Generally, they select the soft rubble bars at the tails of pools in big water—all along the main stem itself and in the lowest few miles of the West Branch. The lower pH water of the East Branch somehow fails to attract them.

While brown trout have certainly altered the nature of the Neversink fishery, they probably haven't added much to it. If, as they say, it takes four pounds of stream food to build a pound of wild trout flesh, the upper Neversink should be producing about the same poundage of trout per mile as it did before the introduction. However, since the browns preempt the food-rich lies, the brookies now have to be fewer in number and perhaps a bit smaller. On the brighter side, knowing that the next fish you hook could be a high-jumping, eighteen-inch brown does pump up your pulse rate a bit.

7

Enemies

Trout, especially the larger browns, are the reigning carnivores of the river and, as such, are the top link in the river's food-production chain. No other river resident challenges them. Unfortunately, the pecking order doesn't stop there, because of the superior predators on the land bordering, and in the sky above, the water.

Several species of birds make their living off river fish. Two of the largest, the bald eagle and the osprey, probably concentrate on suckers. There are a lot of these in the river and the adults average about sixteen inches long, or about a pound and a half, and make a substantial meal. Few trout of over nine inches lie in vulnerable places during the bright hours when these large raptors patrol the river, and the small fry that do are probably not worth a stoop from birds with six- to eight-foot wingspans.

The equally large great blue herons are another matter. They'll stand rock-still for hours in slow, one- to nearly two-foot-deep water, waiting for a fish to cruise within range. They, too, are daylight hunters and usually get only smallish fish. However, I have twice caught trout in the ten- to twelve-inch category with fresh stab wounds nearly an inch deep in their backs, so herons are occasionally lucky enough to get a shot at decent-sized fish. I am certain they can easily swallow as big a fish as they're likely to catch. In Florida, I have seen the semitame herons that work the fishing-boat docks gulp down two-foot-long sea trout with one bob of their necks.

Kingfishers work the shallows, diving headlong from tree branches overhanging the river. Because of their relatively small size and the nature of the shallows they hunt, they probably get a lot of bait minnows, but they also cull some of the young-of-the-year trout. Since there seems to be a surplus of these, I don't consider kingfishers a serious threat to the fishery.

American mergansers, on the other hand, are truly destructive and far too numerous—especially in late summer when the several pairs that nest in the Valley have raised their broods of eight to ten young to maturity. These flocks swim around in the pools, diving under to chase, and usually catch, fish. They are said to eat a quarter of their body weight each day. Since they weigh in at about two and a half pounds, that adds up to a lot of trout.

Then, too, mergansers take the scarcer, medium-sized fish which kingfishers can't. I once found on the riverbank a merganser that had just choked to death on a trout. The cause of death was easy to diagnose because the fish's tail protruded from the bird's bill. That trout measured a full ten inches and, from this evidence, I assume that mergansers can swallow trout up to nine inches long, or most two-year-old fish.

Mergansers used to be considered vermin—they're virtually inedible—but since they're now classified as game birds with a closed season and bag limits, their numbers are ominously increasing. In the Valley, during the summer, one occasionally hears gunfire—nearly always only a shot or two, so it's clearly not clay-target shooting. Apparently, some people are acting as vigilantes and turning these marauders into "good mergansers." If you're even imagining that I could kill one of these soft, brown-eyed, (trout-gulping) creatures— shame on you!

Beasts as well as birds are fond of trout, and a few dine exclusively on fish. River otters are the largest animals that fall into this category. Fortunately, they're restless travelers that space their kills. They may dine on a fish—always fastidiously leaving the head—and not catch their next meal until they're several miles away, so they're not likely to make as much of a dent in any one pool as a family of mergansers can.

There are only a few otters in the Valley, anyway: one, possibly two, breeding pairs. They are extremely shy and seldom seen. Their presence is usually detected only by the roundish pugmarks in sand or mud, the head and skeleton of a good-sized fish left on a rock, or by the toboggan-tracks they leave in the snow after playfully sliding down an incline with their legs retracted.

Their smaller relatives, the mink, are more numerous and some-what less secretive. While they, too, tend to keep well out of sight they can, on occasion, become quite cheeky. More than once mink have loped along the bank of a pool I was fishing, dived into the water, appeared seconds later with a decent trout, and proceeded to devour it on the spot only thirty feet away. I'll admit they watched me warily the whole time, but that's still a brazen performance. I got the distinct impression that they didn't think much of my fly rod and were showing me how the job was properly done.

Raccoons relish fish, too, but they're poor swimmers so they forage from the bank or in the shallows. In summer they can take trout readily from small, nearly dried-up brooks, but their river-take is mostly crawfish or the occasional dead trout whose corpse has been washed into the shallows.

Of course the most efficient trout predator of all doesn't fly through the air or plunge in from the riverbank. Man, with fly, lure, worm, or worse, can virtually wipe out a fishery, which is what happened in the early history of the Neversink. Even a solitary angler, with persistence, can decimate a stretch of stream—as I discovered to my chagrin that first year in the Valley.

Although trout will play musical chairs in spring and again at fall spawning-time, they are essentially residents for most of the open season. If the majority of good ones are cleaned out of a particular section, it will offer slim pickings for the rest of that year.

Since the Neversink lies on the edge of America's most densely populated area, all riparian owners feel the need to post their property. A few have their own part-time patrollers who spot-check at fairly regular intervals. Some contiguous owners band together and pay someone to make an occasional sweep during the weekdays when they're away. No system is airtight. Probably the highly visible posters and the widespread knowledge that most of the water is patrolled is about the only affordable deterrent.

The situation is certainly better than it was a few years ago when several properties were left unposted. I now catch only two or three "uninvited guests" on my water each year, and these are usually vacationers from out of state who know little about postings and even less about trout fishing.

How many *don't* I catch? I think I can make a surprisingly accurate count. Each weekend, while fishing, I examine the streambed ahead of me for scuff marks and check sandy patches for boot prints. Years ago, I laid a false track down the stream and checked it every day to note the rate of healing. Boots and wading shoes scrape the algae off rocks and it takes a predictable time for this to grow back—about a week at summer temperatures, ten days to two weeks in early spring and fall. On the few occasions when I find unauthorized tracks, I can now say with some certainty that I had a visitor last Wednesday. In addition, I've learned to tell whether my guest was bait fishing or fly casting.

Each type of angler takes a distinctly different path through a river. Just call me Sherlock Wright.

I ran across my most glamorous poacher during my second season on the West Branch. I was sauntering upstream to catch the evening hatch when I spotted an angler standing on a rock in midstream. The first thing that caught my eye was his fishing attire. From bottom to top, this consisted of heavy English wading brogues, neatly pressed Bermuda shorts, white button-down shirt, and Madras jacket. Then I noticed he was wielding an exquisite little Payne bamboo rod adorned with a vintage Hardy reel. Far and away the most piss-elegant poacher I'd ever seen.

From fifty feet behind him, I began with my usual soft opening. "Any luck?"

He turned toward me and I could then guess his age as about fifteen.

"I'm terribly sorry, sir. Did I step in in front of you?" The accent was purest Groton.

"No," I said, stalling for time. Then I went into my usual question number two. "Do you fish here often?"

"Oh no. This is my first time, actually. I was invited over for the afternoon."

I sat down on a rock to sort things out and finally it came to me. The Queen of the West Bank's son had told me he'd gone to school with the grandson of one of our famous, nineteenth century robber barons, and added that he'd been meaning to invite him and his sons over to fish since they summered in a nearby valley. Obviously, a great-grandson had accidentally started in a half mile below the mark.

"Are you absolutely certain I'm not hogging your favorite spot, sir?"

"Sure, my favorite pool's quite a way downriver," I said. Then, as I headed in that direction, I added, "Good fishing."

I won't reveal the family involved because I'm not a name-dropper. And I seem to have another minor virtue: I certainly know my place, don't I?

At the very opposite end of the scale was a scruffy-looking eighteen-year-old I later found drowning a worm right in front of my house on the main stem. I strolled down and went through my usual genteel routine until I got to gambit number five, which runs, "Did you happen to notice any posters on the trees as you came downriver?"

"Yep, I saw 'em, but I don't know what they said 'cause I can't read."

I understand that ignorance is no excuse before the law, but he might have a point. I wrote down his name and license number anyway, and made it quite clear that he should leave immediately—which he did.

When I checked him out a couple of weeks later, I learned he was a member of a large, not-too-prosperous family that worked a hilltop farm a few miles away. I was also told that he'd just graduated from the local high school.

Feeling I'd been had, I belatedly turned him in to the local justice of the peace for processing. The next weekend I got a call from the JP telling me that my case couldn't be pursued because the culprit had recently left the state for Colorado. "And get this," he added. "His family says he's out there taking courses to pass his game warden's exam."

Well, if it takes one to catch one, he'll make a damned good warden, too.

8

The Life Blood

Despite all the time I had spent in this valley, it wasn't until my fifth season, or second summer downriver, that I witnessed—or, more accurately, experienced—a major flood in progress. That's not to say there hadn't been six or eight floodings of varying severity during that period; the Neversink seems to overflow its banks at least once a year. But either I had been in the city during peak flows or, when I was in the Valley, the river had crested after dark and receded substantially by daybreak.

Rain started coming down in cauldrons late one July afternoon and hammered on the roof steadily until the next morning. My neighbor's rain gauge recorded over nine inches during that period. Since it takes some eight hours for the Neversink to crest after the midpoint of any rainstorm, I expected the river to keep rising until about eight o'clock that morning.

I had been roused at first light by a noise more like a hurricane than the rush of water. The low, hissing roar seemed to surround the house, pouring in from all sides, rather than coming from the river itself.

I stepped out onto the small terrace in front of the house to get a more panoramic view of the river. The waters had overwhelmed the five-foot bank on the far side and were lapping at my signs posted on the tree trunks. The level, forested floodplain extended beyond that for nearly a half mile and all of it had to be under a good three feet of water. With that volume of flow moving through woods and fields, any estimate of the vertical rise in river height would be meaningless.

The scene before me looked more like a section of Amazon rain forest than a mountain river. It was a vast sheet of café au lait, devoid of any contours like rapids or pools. Only the occasional uprooted tree, rafting down the center of the current, gave any clue as to how fast this entire mass was traveling.

The largest of these battering rams had rootballs up to twelve feet in diameter, and when these hung up on the river bottom, the tree would briefly seesaw before hurrying on downcurrent, branches first. These juggernauts were redistributing tons of rock and gravel to new sites, and wherever they hung up against a bank they tore out others to join their destructive ranks. How any living creature—aquatic insect or fish—could survive such an onslaught amazes me. I issued strict orders to the children to stay well back from the river and confined our dog to the house.

River-sized torrents of water ripped out the pavement in several sections of the Valley road, rendering it nearly impassable. This didn't rank as a hundred-year flood—the older residents claimed the one in 1928 was higher—but it came close. Other Catskill rivers had also flooded, but not nearly as destructively as the Neversink.

Back in the city the following week, I went to a map store and picked up the Geodetic Quadrangles covering most of the Catskills to find out if some trick of topography caused the Neversink's instability. I laid the maps out on the floor, scotch-taped them together, and with a felt-tipped marker outlined the perimeter of the river's drainage basin.

The resulting picture looked like a fat, wobbly, paddle-tennis racquet, quite narrow down near the reservoir and swelling out from midsection to top. Due to the vagaries of the surrounding hills, all the larger tributaries entered its branches in the top half of the catchment area. Of course, the fact that for most of its length the upper Neversink is two separate rivers added to this top-heavy pattern. Still, this odd shape was in itself no cause for extra flooding. It was merely a quirk of geography that only a few small brooks fed into the lower river just before it emptied into the reservoir.

This five-mile-long body of water, plugged in 1954, was probably named more for the township than the river, since neighboring Asho-kan, Pepacton, and Downsville reservoirs also reflect place, rather than river, names. The word Neversink, however, must have taunted the fates, or at least the engineers of the Bureau of Water Supply. The original town site now lies under 160 feet of water.

It was all a big misunderstanding though. "Neversink" doesn't mean what it says. It's just a phonetic form of the Indian word for this river, which meant "water between highlands." That pretty much de-scribes *any* mountain river and demonstrates that the Indians probably weren't such colorful, imaginative characters after all.

Other features on the maps at hand gave far more revealing clues. The upper reaches of both the Beaver Kill and the Willowemoc, which also appeared on the quadrangles, each held several ponds, bogs, and plateaus that would slow up and meter out runoff. The Neversink drainage had none of these. In fact, in most of its upper watershed, the twenty-foot contour lines were packed tightly together.

The next weekend, I got in my car and headed upvalley over the partly repaired road—this time not to look over the river but to examine the surrounding hills. In the uppermost five miles of valley, where the basin area was widest, steep hills towered over the riverbed. It looked like perfect territory for downhill ski trails and for expert racers. In heavy rainfall these slopes would sluice water into the Never-sink almost as quickly as those concrete catchments you see on Caribbean islands.

Further data on the Neversink area were easy to pick up because the water supply people had made exhaustive studies and kept detailed records both before and after building their dam. For instance, the river, where it enters the reservoir, carries the drainage from 91.8 square miles. However, since its basin starts high up in the southwestern Catskills, it receives more than its regional share of rainfall. Storm clouds from both the south and west—the most prevalent wind directions—are forced upwards and cooled on the mountain slopes, causing them to drop extra moisture. The result is an average precipitation of sixty-five inches a year or half again as much as the forty-three inches not-too-distant New York City expects.

Hydrologists say that only 27 percent of annual rainfall is carried off by rivers. Some trickles down to renew deep aquifers. Quite a bit simply evaporates. Most of the rest, especially in summer, is sucked up by growing vegetation and transpired through leaves back up into the atmosphere to fall again as rain in some other area.

This still leaves the main river with a mean flow of 1,200 gallons per second, or about 100 million gallons per day. The metropolis doesn't get all this water, despite its dam. Sizable quantities have to be released as mandated compensation flow to recreate some semblance of a waterway in the old riverbed below. This flow, discharged from the very bottom of the reservoir, is extremely cold and creates a smaller, but far more stable, public fishery for another ten or fifteen miles below the dam.

That figure of 1,200 gallons per second may be meaningful to the water-supply people, but since it's only an average it doesn't tell you much about the river's size or flow at any given moment. Rain-fed rivers are extremely volatile—the Neversink especially so. When several weeks go by without significant precipitation, as they often did in the mid-1960s, flows have been known to shrink to a stingy fifty-five gallons per second. At the other extreme, volumes as high as 130,000 gallons per second, or about 2,500 times minimum flow, were estimated during one flood.

This rapid runoff has an additional effect: Rainwater doesn't sink in deep or travel very far through humus or topsoils. Water is known as the universal solvent because it dissolves more types of substances and absorbs greater quantities of them than any other liquid. But the longer the contact, the greater the absorption.

Short and rapid travel of rainwater into the river means that there's little time to buffer the natural acidity of raindrops, to pick up nutrients from organic matter, or to leach enriching minerals out of rocks and soils. As a result, Neversink water is as clear as aquavit. But it is also, with the possible exception of the upper Rondout Creek, the least fertile river water in the Catskills.

Over and above this topographical handicap, there's an even more fundamental reason why Neversink water lacks richness: the geological one. The rock strata that make up the Catskills are virtually devoid of common fertilizer minerals such as potash, nitrates, and sulfates. Nourishing carbonates are almost totally lacking as well.

This poverty of enriching elements was inherited from the older, mineral-deficient mountains that towered to the east 350 million years ago in what is now western Massachusetts. Over millions of years, wind, rain, and frost eroded these Himalaya-sized peaks, and most of the resulting particulates were carried westward and deposited in alluvial fans where the runoff slowed up. As these deltas grew in height and width, they merged and formed a huge tilted mesa several thousand feet high in the east and sloping off gradually to the west.

Today's Catskills were sculptured by erosion out of this high plateau of recycled debris. The original, contributing mountains to the east were overly generous. Today's three-thousand-foot, mineral-poor Berkshires are the remnant stubs of peaks that were once ten times that high.

Another major event, the Ice Age, played a significant role in forming the Catskills. Since they lie only a hundred miles north of the deepest penetration of the ice sheet, they weren't subjected to as much grinding and toppling as the Adirondacks were, but they were certainly carved up by it. The main glacier detoured to the east down the huge gully of the already existing Hudson Valley, but fingers of it pushed through Catskill valleys, alternately gouging out land and depositing rocks and soils bulldozed and transported from other areas to the north. As a result, the soil map of this area looks like a crazy quilt. As luck would have it, the patches deposited in the Neversink Valley are among the poorest and least fertile in the region.

Since the upper Valley is sparsely inhabited, it also receives few nutrients from detergents or treated human wastes from cesspools and septic tanks. In fact, the water is so pure that thirsty fishermen feel safe drinking it, and I have never heard of anyone becoming ill from doing this.

The late Harry Darbee, one of the Catskill's legendary flytiers, once told me a story that underlines this point. Back in the early 1930s when he was a young man, Harry drove his Model T over to Hewitt's place on the Neversink to enlist the great man's help. After persuading Hewitt to accompany him back to the Beaver Kill, Harry led him to Junction Pool at Roscoe where, until recently, a large pipe emerged from the ground just above the river's edge. Out of it ran an intermittent stream of off-color water punctuated by odd pieces of toilet paper. It was obviously the outflow of the town's sewage system and it was, equally obviously, untreated.

"Mr. Hewitt," Harry pleaded, "nobody will listen to a young flytier like me, but you're America's most famous fisherman and they'll sure listen to you. You've got to get the authorities to make the town stop pouring raw sewage into the river. They'll kill every last trout."

Hewitt's quick response shook the young man. "I certainly will *not!* Sewage, in limited amounts, is one of the world's richest fertilizers. I've always wondered why the insect hatches over here are so much bigger than they are on the Neversink and I've finally found out why."

Clearly, it would be impractical—and quite certainly illegal—to dump raw sewage into a river that was the gem of the New York City water supply. But it made me wonder if other types of nutrients were lacking as well. I sent for a small kit that tested for acidity/alkalinity and soon turned up some revealing figures. The East Branch registered a stingy pH of 5.7. The West Branch was a far healthier 6.5. And the main stem, a few miles below, was up to 6.8 or just a hair below the neutral figure of pH 7.

In contrast, the more productive Beaver Kill and Willowemoc next door were slightly alkaline at pH 7.2 and the food-factory Delaware River, into which they flowed, showed an even better 7.4. New York State fishery biologists confirmed my hunch that, all other factors being equal, the higher the pH, the greater the food production.

I recalled having read an article in a British fishing magazine a few years back about improving fisheries by spreading powdered limestone in streambeds, and dug through my stack of back issues until I found it. I wrote a letter to the editor, asking for more specifics and requesting that he pass it on to the author, whose address was unknown to me.

Brits must be more punctilious with correspondence than we are, for in no time I received all the information I had requested from the late Frank Sawyer, angler, author, and river keeper on the Hampshire Avon near Stonehenge. Part of his long letter went as follows: "Carbonate of lime which, of course, is the basis of both chalk and limestone, has been used with great success in the upper Avon. Aquatic life of all kinds has increased to a degree of abundance far beyond what was anticipated. Those to benefit most are animals of the crustacea and mollusk families and these are the types of food animals which are of a satisfying and body-building nature for trout.

"Here we try to arrange matters so that an even dressing of lime is given to the river bed twice yearly, in April and in late July. To effect this, the chalk powder must first be brought into suspension and the applications made at times when a fall out from suspension can take place without the water carrying away too much downstream. You might try two, or perhaps three, tons of powder per acre of water for a start and then judge accordingly. If this does no good, I can assure you it will do no harm even if you use ten or even twenty times that amount."

The voice of experience carried authority, but I had to remind myself that the Avon was an extremely stable chalk stream. The earlier loss of my jerry-built dam and my recent viewing of a full-fledged flood had dispelled any notions I may have had about the Neversink's docility. I could now predict that the next flood—perhaps even modest spate—would flush any fine limestone (plus, perhaps, tons of heavier rocks and gravel) out of my river bottom and into the reservoir below. However, the suggestion to add lime by some method was so persuasive that I decided a pilot project on one of the smaller, and presumably more manageable, tributaries might be worth a try.

I outlined my plan to the Queen of the West Branch and asked her permission to dump limestone gravel into Low Fall Brook—an upriver tributary six to eight feet wide that ran through her property. "Of course," she characteristically replied. "And wouldn't it be exciting if it worked?"

I ordered a twenty-ton truckload of white limestone gravel from the nearest source, a quarry in northern New Jersey, and had it dumped across the bed of the brook, just below where it passed under the road and about a hundred yards above its confluence with the West Branch. After some shoveling and raking, it blocked the entire stream channel with a berm fifteen feet wide, three feet high, and several feet deep. It backed up some water, but since its chunks were only about the size of walnuts, all the flow trickled through the interstices a couple of feet below the top.

The water below ran chalky-white all day as the stream rinsed away the lime powder that had been part of the truckload. The stream's pH had been 5.7 before the application. I waited until the next weekend before taking a reading, knowing that the first flows would give an unrealistically high figure.

My testing kit registered 6.3! I had raised it .6 pH, which may not sound like much, but the pH scale is a logarithmic one and the figure meant that now several times as many nourishing carbonates were in the water.

I retested on subsequent weekends and the pH level held up at between 6.2 and 6.3. As the weeks went by, my dam seemed to shrink a bit and, coincidentally, I noticed that several front-door paths to village houses had suddenly turned startlingly white. Being a man of extreme delicacy, I didn't walk over to grab a sample, but the gravel looked disturbingly familiar. Apparently a small local tax was being levied on my supply of limestone, but I considered the project a resounding success despite this attrition.

I then calculated that if seven other sizable upstream tributaries were also limed, about 50 percent of the river volume could be enriched and the pH of the lower river could be raised to the fly-rich Beaver Kill's level of 7.2.

I drew maps, laid plans, figured costs, dreamed dreams. I felt I had stumbled onto the salvation of all the underproductive streams and rivers in the Northeast. It might not win me a Nobel prize, but state and private fishery experts would surely troop to my door for advice as they once had, back in the 1920s and 1930s, to the great Edward R. Hewitt's.

During the last week of August, while I was hard at work in the city, I read in *The New York Times* that a parade of freak thunderstorms had hit parts of the Catskills, causing severe flash flooding. Had the Neversink been hit or missed? I fidgeted at the office and tossed and turned at night.

Traffic out of New York City that Friday evening was atrocious and it was pitch-dark when we finally reached the Valley. Another night of uncertainty. I set the alarm for dawn, and headed upriver before sunup. Litter high up on the banks indicated there had, indeed, been flooding. I wasn't expecting any pleasant surprises, but when I reached the brook, I was appalled. The small streambed was in tatters, littered with undermined and stranded trees and studded with huge, unfamiliar boulders. I couldn't see a trace of my limestone.

Later that day I walked the lower brookbed and a half mile down the West Branch, immediately below, searching for pieces of the glittering white stones. To this day, I have never found so much as one pea-sized chunk from that entire twenty tons.

In this run-amok watershed, apparently even a mild-looking tributary could turn into one of those monstrous firehoses that placer miners use to demolish entire hillsides. If you want to bet that this rather expensive project hasn't been repeated, you've put money on a sure thing.

9

The Way of a Stream

My pile of limestone wasn't the only streambed feature rearranged by that flash flood. Tons of other rocks and gravel were swept up, juggled, and redeposited in new locations. Runs and riffles were lengthened, shortened, moved upstream and down. Some familiar pools filled in. A few new ones were created.

When water levels dropped back to near normal, I started out on an inspection tour of my home water. Before a post-flood trip like this one, my anxiety always matches that of the hero in that classic suspense story, "The Lady or the Tiger?" Remember? He was sentenced to open either of two doors—behind one stood a lovely damsel and behind the other a ravenous tiger.

The head of my first pool, just below the house, had been gouged slightly deeper and acquired a couple of new boulders from the hillside, but to cancel out this gain, the tail end of it had been shallowed out by deposits of gravel cutting the length of the lower brook-trout flat in half.

The series of three pocket pools just around the bend had been slightly resculptured, too. One was longer and deeper, another shorter and shallower. But so far I felt my water had broken even.

Cliff Pool, below, had been altered dramatically, though. It was now only two-thirds as wide as previously because the left side opposite the cliff had been filled in with rubble. Mercifully, the deep channel and the lies under the cliff overhang were as clean as they had been and probably held as many trout as ever. However, this pinching of the waist of the pool hurried the current through faster, which meant that when the river rose a foot or so a prime section would become unfishable.

Cliff Pocket appeared unaltered, as did the unproductive riffle it flowed into. The next long flat was another matter: It had been trashed, literally. Floodwaters had dropped a foot or more of sand, gravel, and small rocks where the current-speed slackened, leaving the area nearly featureless. Only the tops of a few recognizable boulders poked above this rubble deposit. The entire area was now too thin to interest even a small brook trout.

There were changes in the flat below this, too. The channel running along the steep right bank had silted in completely, while the left-hand one had been improved. An old, dry riverbed—one that doesn't come into play until the water rises four or five feet, and which cuts an overland hypotenuse through the woods—rejoins the river here, and it had apparently carried enough flow in this near-record flood to gouge the bed a foot deeper. The run at the bottom of my water looked about the same. All in all, I had to figure that my fishery had lost about 20 percent of its good holding capacity.

While it is undoubtedly true that the Lord giveth and the Lord taketh away, it has been my experience that when He reorganizes riverbeds he seems a bit stronger in the taketh-away department.

During my years in the Valley I'd made an amateur study of river behavior and had come to realize that floods, though temporarily damaging—they can depress an entire season's fishing—can be long-term blessings in disguise. They are the master builders of a stream's contours, and it is their force that digs out pools, scours channels into deep runs, and creates pocket water in rapids studded with boulders too big to be dislodged.

Then too, we have to thank floods for making the riverbed hospitable to aquatic insects, which are the trout's major food source. If underwater rocks weren't periodically flushed, or even rolled over, they would soon become cemented together with silt and sand deposits, leaving no interstices for mayfly nymphs and caddisworms to live or hide in. Rivers like Connecticut's Farmington, and even the Neversink itself below the dam, both of which depend on metered flows from impoundments and therefore rarely flood, have stream bottoms of either sand deposits or small, cemented cobbles that are virtual insect wastelands.

If you examine a river from an unusual perspective, it will tell you most of the rules of running-water behavior. The trick is to view it with the eye of a surveying instrument, visualizing it at levels five to six feet higher than normal flows.

A typical example would be the water immediately below bridge abutments. At average water level these pillars usually emerge from the streambed near or even back from the water's edge. But raise the river six feet vertically in your mind's eye and you'd see that the river, swelling over its banks above, would be severely pinched in the bridge area. This would greatly speed up the flow in that section, and the faster the water, the larger the rocks it can pick up and transport downstream. That's why there's nearly always a pool, or at least a long, deep pocket below bridges.

A vertical plunge of water also picks up speed at floodtime, gaining in digging and rock-moving power. Abysses below dams bear testimony to this force. So do deeply scoured holes below large boulders that may emerge above the surface in low flows, but which have several feet of water tumbling over their tops during floods.

A minor variation of this phenomenon occurs at the bottom of a steep run or riffle where land contours level out. Water running down a slope not only picks up speed, which adds digging power, but also tends to keep flowing in the same plane, digging into the suddenly leveled streambed. This explains, in part, why the heads of pools are nearly always the deepest parts—gradually shallowing out toward the tail, where material dredged from above is deposited by slowed currents no longer able to transport it.

Another key principle is also easy to observe. Water flowing over an underwater, linear obstruction—whether a submerged log or a natural bar—will abruptly change direction and flow at precisely 90 degrees to that structure. In other words, if a log is wedged across a streambed at, say, a 45-degree angle, the left end being downstream and the right upstream, the flow below it, as in the case of my aforementioned Cliff Pocket, will be shunted to the right at exactly 45 degrees.

Since I'd decided to undertake major stream-improvement projects, I thought it wise to look into the literature on running water in case it might tell me things the river itself had forgotten to. I discovered that much of this material dealt with water's movement through pipes and conduits, which seemed logical since most of the water we use reaches us through such conveyors. A lot also dealt with the channeling and straightening of streams—an abomination carried out to minimize flooding in low-lying areas and one especially dear to the hearts of the Corps of Engineers.

I did spot one extremely helpful article on natural rivers in *Scientific American*. This was a piece by Luna B. Leopold and W. B. Langbein on the laws of meanders. Their studies showed that a river, regardless of size, tended to form one of these serpentine loops every time it had traveled three to four times its width. Of course, rivers and streams form true meanders only where the stream gradient is virtually level, but there was a useful corollary in their findings.

The authors went on to postulate that in steeper, rain-fed rivers this pattern appeared to repeat itself in a slightly different manner. They found strong evidence that the pool-riffle sequence in such flows also tended to occur at predictable intervals: namely, once in every five to seven widths of travel. I could find little confirmation of this law on my own immediate stretch of water—the vagaries of intervening hills and land contours seemed more in control—but I tucked it away as a useful precept. Since my water averaged thirty-five- to forty-five-feet wide on average, I might be fighting the laws of nature if I tried to jink or jockey it more than once every 200 to 250 feet.

I also gathered some down-to-earth stream-improvement booklets. These contained diagrams and photographs of recommended structures and added good advice on where to position them.

They warned to avoid areas where the riverbed wandered through a floodplain lest your labor- or cost-intensive structure end up on dry land, many useless feet from the new stream channel. They also advised diverting the current only against a strong, permanent bank. Shunting it over toward a weak, eroding shoreline can defeat your purpose—widening rather than pinching the riverbed. And lastly, they pointed out that all river-improvement devices (except dams, of course) were most effective when installed on the bank nearest the main thread of the current.

For these reasons I decided that the floodplain water near my house would best be left alone until it had dug a deeper, permanent channel anchored by firmly-rooted trees along both banks. While that should eventually happen, it might not come to pass during my lifetime.

I therefore took my business downstream, beyond the bend where bankside trees told me the river had run that course for over fifty years. Cliff Pool, Cliff Pocket, and the three good pocket pools appeared to be taking care of themselves, so I passed them by, too. The long, featureless riffle directly below, however, struck me as a waste of river yardage.

I could put a dam in there, but that would cost many thousands of dollars, and confronting flows head-on can, in some situations, be self-defeating. A dam creates slow water upstream, inviting deposits of sand and gravel to fill in that newly-created pool, and eventually turns it into a featureless—and fishless—section. The only permanent gain from a dam that you can count on is the plunge pool directly below it, and on a fish-per-dollar basis that just didn't add up.

On a river as volatile as the Neversink it would be far wiser, I thought, to harness the power of floodwaters. I would borrow from the principle of jujitsu, which involves converting your opponent's strength to your advantage.

The left bank of the long riffle offered the most promising site for improvement because the main current, ricocheting off the rock wall of Cliff Pocket, flowed to that side. It would also be safer to anchor logs by burying them in a rubble bank than to try to pin them to the opposing rock cliff. I chose to construct a low cribbing that would pinch the river a bit and create a scour along its length.

A cribbing is simply a log cage that confines hundreds or thousands of stones and rocks and keeps them from washing away during floods. It is commonly used to pinch or divert currents or to stabilize an eroding bank. Properly designed, constructed, and maintained, one should last from twenty-five to fifty years.

Essential to a cribbing's longevity is the use of rot-resistant logs. Hemlock, cedar, oak, and a few less common trees can get wet and dry out again and again over extended periods without rotting. Wood like white pine, on the other hand, can take this treatment for only three or four years before getting soft and pulpy. Fortunately, there was a dense grove of medium-sized hemlocks on the steep, opposing bank, which I could use as a handy source of materials.

After cutting and preparing the required logs came the task of digging a sizable trench into the bank at the top end of the site to accommodate the first tie-logs. This slot had to be cut by pick, shovel, and sweat nearly ten feet into the bank at a 30-degree angle, sloping downstream so that flotsam in floodtime would easily slide off these key logs. All the displaced rocks and gravel had to be piled conveniently nearby to be used as fill-in once the anchoring timbers were in place. It was brutal work because the sides of the slot tended to cave in, and to dig that distance, and well below the water level, meant removing far more rocks and rubble than I'd anticipated.

Shortly after excavation began, a blessing in the guise of my brother showed up for a week's visit, and he soon became as involved in this project as I was. By working in relay and spelling each other, we finished the trench and had the timbers in place, one on top of the other and securely buried, after three full days of straining and cursing.

The peonage of digging wasn't over yet. It took us another full day to dig a forty-foot-long slot to sink the lower logs of the outer cribbing as deeply as possible. After that, the task of log-cabin-cutting, morticing, and spiking to finish the frame, and then running smaller supporting stringers from the outer logs inward to the bank, seemed almost like rest and recreation.

What we had created was a forty-foot-long cage, two logs high, that started at the upstream bank and slightly angled out into the river for the first log length of twenty feet. Then a matching set of twenty-footers, morticed smoothly into the first pair, jutted out into the river at a slightly sharper angle, increasing the current-pinch by ten to twelve feet. The downstream end of the cribbing was enclosed by two more superposed timbers tied into the bank at an obtuse angle. This increased the amount of fill required but was necessary to ensure that floodwaters pouring over the low structure would be shot out toward center stream, away from the vulnerable bank. The top of this frame was about six inches above water level and would end up a foot or more higher when properly ballasted.

After we'd pinned the structure down with large rocks on the interior stringers to secure it in case of high water, I declared amnesty for what remained of the week, and we stood back to admire our handiwork. In a burst of gratitude, I named it the "W.W.W. Cribbing" in honor of my brother's initials.

To initiate and encourage the desired scour, I picked up as much ballast as I could from the area four or five feet outside the cribbing. Naturally I tried to recruit help for this seemingly endless task, but most weekend guests I found to be less than enthusiastic. I then tried to enlist my preteenaged children to help out by pitching in the numerous smaller rocks.

"Who wants to play the rock game?" got them started eagerly enough, but by the end of an hour I was down to my last co-worker, and he seemed to be looking for a reprieve. Despite what those dragooned laborers may tell you, I ended up tossing 99 percent of that fill with my own two hands.

In September, we had our first high water—a miniflood of four to five feet. A few days later I made my usual bated-breath inspection tour and discovered that not only had the cribbing survived intact, but the slot of river bottom I'd destabilized by scavenging for ballast had scoured out nearly a foot deeper. The water right off the logs was waist-deep and the bottom logs, now a good foot off the stream bottom, provided many of those mysterious grottos large trout are so fond of.

That night I phoned my brother in Seattle and described the new wonders in my best imitation of a play-by-play announcer. After an unbroken string of failures, I finally had a solid winner—at least for the time being.

10

The High Cost of Overhead

The next spring brought with it the usual snowmelt flood, but it wasn't the punishing sort that overwhelmed roadways and threatened bridges. The cribbing weathered it surprisingly well and all logs stayed in place. Apparently, the streamlined shape of the structure helped it to shrug off powerful currents.

However, some rock ballast had been lost at the lower end of the cribbing. It had scoured deepest where it jutted out farthest into the river and pinched the current most, and the lower log was now two feet above the new streambed and half the nearby rock and rubble had been sucked out from underneath it. Fortunately this damage could be repaired with some strenuous work once the water receded and warmed.

The structure had not only created a new deep along the logs, but an additional bonus I hadn't anticipated—a trench that extended some twenty feet downstream from its bottom end. While this deepened water seldom held good fish during the bright of day, some under-log residents drifted back into it at dusk, lengthening the fishing area.

I was mildly disappointed that my deflector hadn't shunted the current over toward the opposite bank as expected. The extra water now flowing along the logs and just below had apparently created a dominant current-thread that hugged the other side all the way down to the end of the riffle. This is one of the reasons why stream-improvement manuals recommend starting work at the top of the stretch of water to be improved and adding downstream structures as needed, rather than vice versa. It would come as an unpleasant surprise if your newest structure, constructed upriver, shot the current away from, rather than toward, a cribbing immediately below.

Once the hot, fishless afternoons of summer set in, I faced up to my repair chores. First, rocks of all sizes within several feet of the depleted area inside the logs had to be tossed well up onto the bank to clear out the space nearest the bottom log. This was mindless drudgery, but if I worked into a rhythm of motion, the way slaves hoeing fields once must have, the minutes and hours slid by without anguish.

Next I crowbarred boulders out of the adjacent stream bottom and rolled them over near the cribbing. I had to reject any easy ones less than two feet in diameter because that was the size of the gap they had to block, so I selected the biggest ones I could roll underwater. Getting them up a plank ramp and over the top log was a gut-straining, two-man job, and a couple of the biggest rocks never made it.

Once the breach was chinked with boulders, I had to go back up the bank and toss again, returning the laboriously removed ballast to its previous site. By the time I was finished, my hands were as smooth as a Mexican truck tire and down to lean red meat in places.

This staggering expenditure of man-hours had, at least, produced something of value. It had converted a featureless, calf-deep riffle into a long glide three to four feet deep with ideal overhead cover. Trout could tuck in under the logs, unseen by enemies, and eye the current-thread diagonally above for passing insect tidbits. Six or eight good trout—ones twelve- to sixteen-inches long—made this place their summer home.

Water three feet deep is in itself not necessarily a major fish attraction on this clear-water river, and many sections of this depth rarely contain good-sized trout. The secret of my cribbing's success was the ideal overhead cover it also provided. Brown trout may feed in shallow, exposed current-tongues, but they won't take up residence there. Once they've reached maturity, they seek out sunken logs, root snags, undercut rocks, cutbanks, or any type of structure that puts a roof over their heads while they're resting.

The importance of this requirement hadn't been impressed upon me before, but creating cover now became a top priority. I pried up large rock slabs from the stream bottom and wedged rocks under their edges, turning them into low-slung coffee tables. I cut down bushy fifteen-foot pine trees and wired them to underwater boulders. I levered big rocks down steep hillsides, sending them crashing into pools below. Trout appeared out of nowhere to take advantage of these new sanctuaries, but most of my jerry-built improvements lasted a few months at most. The first modest flood knocked down my elevated rock tables and tore the pine trees from their moorings. What I really needed were lies with more permanence—ones where trout could ride out dangerous floods and where they could winter on my property.

So I went back to cribbings and started work on a second one the following summer. This was to be sited on the same side of the river, about 250 feet below the first one and at the top end of the now filled-in flat. I designed it to jut out a bit further into the river—some fifteen feet at the downstream end—hoping it would scour out the rubble deposited by the flood.

The endless hours of digging, cave-ins, and cursing began all over again. But the work went a bit more smoothly now that I had some experience, and this time I got more help. The one child of mine who liked fishing, and several rod-wielding guests, were impressed enough with the fishing the existing cribbing had produced to pitch in from time to time.

The new structure was finished and well filled in before the fall floods, two of which roared through in October. My bated-breath examination after the second and more severe flood revealed that both structures had held up even though the new one hadn't done what I'd expected. It failed to scour the flat back to the old fish-holding rocks, and had merely dug a good channel along the logs the same way the one above had. This couldn't be called a failure, though, because the new structure would probably house at least as many respectable fish as the old flat had.

We were subjected to an even higher flood the following spring, and this revealed a hidden weakness in my cribbings. When water racing over the top of them reached a certain volume and velocity it apparently had the power to suck up and transport smaller, lighter rocks, and about a quarter of the anchoring ballast had been whisked away. What was needed was a lid of large, flat rocks to keep the smaller particles of the rubble fill securely in place. The problem was twofold: Where could I find such material, and how could I handle slabs of that size?

The obvious answer was heavy equipment. I had avoided resorting to this so far, partly because of the expense but also because I would have to submit plans and obtain state permits before bringing machines into the river. This is certainly a wise regulation—for years individuals and town road departments had ripped up riverbeds for fill and gravel—but filing takes a certain amount of time and effort and there's often a long wait for official approval.

I felt that if I had to pay for the transport of a payloader as well as for its actual working hours, I ought to keep it busy for at least a full day building another structure while it was there. I also realized that such a machine could accomplish in a couple of hours what would take me most of a season. I filed plans for a triangular deflector constructed entirely of huge rocks and positioned just above my lower, newest cribbing on the opposite bank. My hope was that this would further pinch the current in that area and flush out the rest of the clogging gravel.

The first job was to locate a source of big rocks. I'd noticed two large fields up the East Branch that served as cow pastures because they contained too many huge stones to make hay mowing possible. When I asked the farmer if he wanted the rocks removed I was told to help myself. I knew that trucking them some five miles would be expensive, but at least the rocks themselves were free.

Next I walked one of the meadows with a can of red paint in hand and left a daub on the rocks that looked useful. Most of the ones I chose weighed from three to five tons, though some of the needed flat ones, only a foot or so thick, were probably nearer a ton.

The first stop for the machinery was up at the meadow. A payloader was flatbedded up there, followed by two medium-sized dump trucks. A payloader, or front-end loader, looks a lot like a bulldozer—it's big, usually yellow, and runs on tank treads or over-sized tires—but it serves an entirely different function. A bulldozer has a flat blade in front that can be raised and lowered and is simply a powerful pusher. A payloader has a huge, toothed bucket up front which can not only be raised and lowered, but rotated as well. In its lowest position it is a powerful digger, and when the bucket is then rotated so that the rim is horizontal, it can carry off the ton or more it has excavated and deposit it, by reverse rotation, at the chosen site.

The two medium-sized dump trucks stood in attendance nearby while the payloader dug out the marked stones. When one truck had been filled—capacity was three to five rocks of this size—it lurched back to the road and on down toward my property.

Fortunately, unloading was the quickest part of this drill. A private dirt road, through which I had a right-of-way, ran along the steep bank overlooking the construction site, and all the truck had to do for final delivery was to back its tail end carefully out over the edge, open its tailgate, hydraulically raise the front of the truckbed, and the rocks would hurtle down the slope into the river sixty feet below. Only two hung up on tree trunks, and they're still there.

The alternating shuttle of trucks kept the front-end loader employed at least half of the time. By noon that part of the operation was finished and the trucks took off for other work and were off my payroll. The payloader then trundled back up onto its flatbed and was transported to the river for the main event.

Placing the flat slabs on the cribbings took only an hour or so, and then the machine turned to digging out the footings for the deflector. This was a vital first step because, as I'd learned from the cribbings, where you pinch the flow severely you get dramatic scouring at floodtime. The huge loader scooped up two or three tons of rubble with each thrust and dumped it to one side for reuse later on.

When about two feet of gravel had been dug out, stable boulders of five hundred pounds or more began to appear—ones not likely to be dislodged by floodwaters. Predigging to the anticipated scour depth is crucial. If you don't, the carefully laid retaining wall of monoliths is likely to topple into the new abyss and the whole structure will collapse like a house of cards.

The loader then placed rocks along the perimeter, the hugest ones on the bottom and the next layer stepped back a bit to ballast their inner ends in case they got deeply undercut. The finished result was a lopsided triangle—the longest leg along the current—that rose a good two feet above water level. Great care was taken in choosing and positioning the rocks so that their outer surfaces were as flush as possible, leaving little chance for logs or rootballs to hang up and yank out key rocks. The operator had the deftness of a diamond cutter. He could nudge or turn a huge problem rock a quarter of an inch at a time with that monstrous, roaring machine. When I mentioned to his helper how impressed I was, he replied, "Hell, he could pick his nose with that bucket if he felt like it." I believed every word of it.

The set-aside rubble was then transferred to inside the rock cage, where it formed a mound three feet higher than the retaining wall. This was capped or riprapped with large rocks pressed in to be nearly flush, especially on the more vulnerable upstream side.

As the payloader waddled back toward its flatbed, I couldn't resist admiring its handiwork. In about half a day it had created what would have taken many hundreds of herniating man-hours to accomplish. Despite a bill of nearly $1,000 (it might come to two or three times that amount today), I was spoiled for life. No more piddling "rock games" for me.

After being sluiced by a couple of minor floods, this secondary pinching did, indeed, clear out most of the flat directly below, but it accomplished more than that. Since this new structure was higher than the cribbing, it diverted a far greater volume of floodwater, which increased its digging power. The result was an awesome blue hole, twenty-five feet long and over six feet deep, just downstream from the apex of the out-jutting triangle. I could barely imagine the size of the trout that would claim this as home territory.

My fishery was, at last, taking shape. Half the length of it couldn't be tinkered with, either because it was too unstable or because it was doing well enough on its own. There was only one area left to be reckoned with—the stretch below my bottom cribbing. The riverbed here was over a hundred feet wide and the fishable channel along the left bank, dug out by an overflow stream during the earlier great flood, was beginning to fill in and become less productive.

That winter I dreamed up all kinds of plans for that section of water, and yet none seemed to provide a practical answer. I would have to block off at least sixty feet of river width to get any significant pinching, and that would be a heroic and confiscatory task. The amount of transported rocks needed to make a triangular structure of that size would obviously be ruinously expensive.

The best I could afford would be a shortcut gamble. If I built a rock structure six feet or so high, it should contain all but exceptional floodwaters and could shunt the current over to the chosen left bank. The only affordable structure would be a wall—not possibly a filled-in triangle—seventy to eighty feet long, starting at the cliff base, sloping gently out into the current at first, then curving out into it until it ended up at a 45-degree angle to the present flow.

First we would have to dig down to a stable, large-rock bottom. Then the lowest layer of rocks would have to be laid to a width of twelve to fifteen feet. At least a double layer would have to be fitted on top of this. And a top row of ultralarge rocks would bring the wall up to a height of six feet or a bit better. Again, the current side of this would have to be fitted in a streamlined manner to prevent uprooted trees from hanging up during floods.

I sent plans to both the state agency and the payloader wizard. The state gave approval on the theory that even if the structure didn't hold up, putting huge rocks into streambeds always helped and couldn't hurt. The structure received its formal name—the Great Wall—months before it had been erected when the payloader man wrote, "If you want to build the Great Wall of China, it's okay with me as long as it's your money."

When you're responsible for a fishery, you tend to keep track of time with a different calendar. The year seems to divide itself into periods of pre- and post-flood conditions. For example, the Great Wall stood there unchanged, just as we'd left it in August, until the miniflood of November. Although the water came up barely five feet, it altered stream contours in that area dramatically. The bottom rocks on the lowest thirty feet of the structure were undercut at least a foot, creating all sorts of dark, fish-holding grottos. And, below the end of the wall, a new pool ten feet by thirty feet had been scoured out to a five-foot depth.

River-time again stood still until the following April, when an average spring flood of six feet continued the good work. The pool was enlarged and deepened to nearly seven feet with a few big rocks left on its bottom. With the hiding holes up under the wall directly above, it soon became one of the most productive stretches on the entire river.

I had now run out of water that needed altering and improving, but I hadn't run out of problems. Every few years a higher-than-average flood poured through with its destructive crop of downed trees, ripping slabs off tops of cribbings or breaching a section of the Great Wall when ultrahigh waters pulled trees complete with rootballs over the top of it. When that happened, I knew I had to get the payloader back in there quickly—certainly before the next flood—or I would probably lose the entire structure.

Even when wind, weather, and water are docile, I can never quite shake off the sense of impending disaster. Like those who reside in the shadow of an active volcano or on top of the San Andreas Fault, I have to live with the anxious certainty that all hell is sure to break loose someday. What I'll never know is precisely *when*.

11

Glorious Food

After several summers devoted to intensive habitat improvement, I now found myself, for the first time, without a major fishery project. Of course after each flush of high water I had to inspect all structures for signs of weakness, loss of ballast, and general wear and tear, but that was a one-hour job and necessary only a few times a year. I felt there must be something more I could be doing to improve my fishing, but for months it escaped me.

I had easily doubled the number of respectable fish living in my water and that was certainly a just reward for all my labors and expenditures. But the unsettling corollary to this was that there were now twice as many fish mouths to feed while the larder remained essentially the same. Would this extra consumption mean slower growth rates for the resident trout? Could it lead to higher mortality since the fish now might have less chance to build up energy reserves for the food-short winter?

Clearly, the river's supply or production of fish food needed looking into. It is a well-known fact that aquatic insects form the trout's staple diet, but I had only a vague idea of how many of these the river was producing.

As a fairly experienced and reasonably well-read fly-fisher, I had some basic knowledge of the various types of stream-bred insects, their appearances, habits, and life cycles, but I'd read nothing on their abundance in freestone streams in general or in the Neversink in particular. I had, however, learned two things: It took four pounds of bug-life to build a pound of trout flesh, and it would take many hundreds, probably thousands, of insects, averaging only five- to ten-millimeters long, to add up to sixteen ounces.

I had also learned or read that 80 percent of this food production took place in the runs and riffles, while the slow-water flats and pools contributed only a stingy 20 percent. This cheered me a bit because over half of my river yardage would have to be classified as fast water. Still, it gave me no idea of the actual volume of food per mile the Neversink produced, nor how much of it was available to the fish.

My first project was to turn over rocks in an approximately square-foot area of shallow riffle, count the insects, and multiply this figure by the estimated square footage of my section of river. But it didn't work. The number of nymphs and larvae clinging to each rock could be estimated, but they quickly scuttled away and hid, so I had no way of knowing how many of those I found under the next rocks were mere repeats.

However, this sampling did help me make a rough comparative measurement. My primitive count led me to expect three or four immature insects on the underside of each fist-sized rock. I then drove over to the Beaver Kill, conducted the same exercise, and found eight to ten insects per rock about par over there. It was easy to conclude that the Beaver Kill produced roughly two to three times the number of insects that the Neversink did, but I still to this day have no idea as to what total numbers and weights would add up to.

I thought I might find some answers in the literature on the ecology of running waters, and hit libraries for texts and pamphlets. I did find some figures on insect counts done by scientists, but most samples were taken from such nutrient-rich, stable streams that they bore little relevance to Neversink conditions. These readings did, however, greatly increase my knowledge of the various orders and even individual species of cold-water aquatic insects.

The most abundant and celebrated of these are the mayflies, or the order of Ephemeroptera—so-named because their adult, or winged, life spans are, indeed, ephemeral, lasting only a day or two. Since most species have a one-year life cycle, this means they spend 363 days grubbing around on underwater rocks for only two days in the air above. Any flier will tell you this is a gruelling amount of ground school for precious little flying time.

Mayflies are favorites with both trout and the fly-fishers who pursue them. They are easy pickings at hatching time as they float downcurrent drying their wings before takeoff, and their high fat content makes them especially nutritious. Classic dry-fly fishing was founded on the habits and shapes of these insects, and over 90 percent of all floating-fly patterns used today are attempted imitations of some mayfly species or other.

Over a thousand species in this order have been identified in North America alone, yet only a handful of these are profuse enough to be important on the Neversink and nearby rivers. While trout may pick off the odd straggler floating by at any time, it is only when hundreds of one of the plentiful mayfly species, responding to some hidden signal, start hatching during a brief period that fish splash and sip all up and down the river and the fly-fisher is certain he's just had a preview of heaven.

Adult, winged mayflies are among the handsomest of insects. That is not to say they're striking and gaudy like some butterflies or tropical beetles. Colors are subtle—mainly grays, browns, yellows, and olives. Shapes are delicate, simple, elegant.

Wings are distinctive, elongated ovals, carried upright and raked slightly to the rear when at rest, like Marconi-rigged sails. Most wings are grayish, though some species show darker mottlings behind an olive or yellow hue. The longish, tubular bodies are of similarly quiet shades and, like the wings, are luminous and translucent. The bodies end with either two or three whisklike tails about the same length as the body. Mayflies are masterpieces of color, harmony, and balance— the understated perfection of the British side-by-side "best gun."

Of course they're not nearly this glamorous during most of their lives underwater. Ephemerids begin life humbly as tiny eggs that soon hatch out into minute, six-legged creatures which immediately start feeding and growing. Since at this stage they have exoskeletons, or at least tough, outer skins, they have to shed these periodically, just as crabs and lobsters do, in order to grow. On average, they moult thirteen times before attaining full growth, but their colors and shapes stay much the same until hatch-out time.

Ripe, full-grown nymphs can usually be identified by the slightly enlarged and darker wing pads on the tops of their thoraces. Once this stage is attained, it may be days, or only hours, before they make the change to winged, adult existence. There appears to be an uncanny unanimity about the taking of this crucial step. For hours on end you won't see a single fly on the water and then, suddenly, a few, then dozens, sometimes hundreds, will appear floating down a pool. What the cue or who the prompter is, nobody knows. It could be water temperature, oxygen levels, light intensity, or some combination of all of the above. The reality is that mayflies are feast-or-famine insects that may appear in swarms for a half hour or up to three hours, and then taper off as abruptly as they began.

Most species simply drift, float, or swim to the water surface above, split open the nymphal shuck, pop up their wings, and after floating for several feet downcurrent, take to the air. Needless to say, at any time during the period after they start this trip and until they become airborne, they are extremely vulnerable to trout. A few species avoid this jeopardy by crawling ashore and hatching out on dry, riverside rocks, but birds patrolling the shoreline may make this a dubious advantage. At least one mayfly—the popular, early-season fly called the Quill Gordon—splits its case before leaving the stream or river bottom and makes its trip to the top while its wings are unfurling—thus, perhaps, shortening its period of helplessness.

Some of the more abundant mayfly species may make daily appearances for two or three weeks. When this occurs, trout quickly get imprinted on a certain size, color, and shape and will accept no substitutes. Under these conditions, even the expert angler who lacks the matching artificial pattern grinds his teeth while he starves in the presence of plenty.

Adults (usually called duns by fly-fishers because most have gray, or dun-colored, wings) that escape the trout below and the swallows above slowly fly to nearby bushes and trees, hiding from hunt-and-peck warblers in the foliage as best they can. During this short period they go through another metamorphosis that is unique among all insects. They shed a filmy outer skin—the dull garment that made them appear dun-colored—from legs, bodies, wings, even tails, and simultaneously alter their shapes. Bodies change color and elongate noticeably, as do front legs and tails. Wings turn glassy. The mayfly is now an agile flying machine instead of a slow, cumbersome dun.

Males appear first over the stream, in small swarms, usually in late evening, hovering over the water, nimbly rising and falling several feet as if riding up and down on invisible, speeded-up elevators. Because of this erratic flight pattern, fly-fishers have always called them "spinners." The slightly larger females soon appear singly, are clasped by a lucky male, and copulation takes place in midair. The female now dips or drops her fertilized eggs onto the water below and minutes later falls dead or dying onto the surface with wings outstretched, forming the shape of a cross. All this may be a transcendental experience for the mayflies, but it strikes me as cruelly brief and a meager ration of ecstasy for an entire lifetime.

As darkness falls, trout get one more crack at the flies they missed earlier. On late-spring and summer evenings, the dimples of trout sipping these helpless, spent-winged flies at the slow, tail ends of pools are a common sight.

Less lovely to look at, perhaps, but nearly as important as sources of trout nutrition, are the caddisflies of the order Trichoptera. Almost everyone is familiar with the few common species readily seen in the slow shallows of rivers and brooks or in the margins of ponds. These rather large specimens are called "stick caddises" because they build their protective cases out of twigs. Children are fascinated by these small, walking log cabins.

While these species are the most visible ones, they represent only a tiny fraction of total caddisfly populations. Over a thousand species have been identified in North America, and most live far more secretive lives.

The majority of caddisflies construct protective cases for themselves, drawing on a wide variety of materials that are glued together with a liquid adhesive the larvae can extrude at will. Each of these species lugs around a distinctive, readily identifiable case made of sand, pebbles, leaf cuttings, grass stems, or even minute snail shells.

Caddisflies do share a few characteristics with mayflies. Most, though not all, are vegetarians. Most also complete a life cycle every twelve months and hatch out into their final, winged state in large, nearly simultaneous flushes called "hatches" by fly-fishers. But, in most ways, caddises are distinctly different beasts.

First, their lumbering larvae are far less mobile than mayfly nymphs, and either creep slowly along the bottom nibbling algae or stay completely immobile, relying on the currents to bring them their daily bread. Some don't bother to build cases at all, but hide, naked, under rocks or in crevices where they spin small nets like tightly woven spider's webs to trap passing food items.

All caddis larvae are soft-bodied, so they grow from their tiny beginnings to full size without shedding. They do have to keep enlarging and elongating their cases, though, otherwise they'd outgrow their portable living rooms.

When they have attained full size, caddis larvae undergo an extra life stage before hatching. For several weeks before hatch-out they seal off most of the open end of their case for protection and enter a semidormant, pupal form. During this transformation they usually change color and shape, and the vestigal wings and long antennae—totally lacking in the larvae—now become prominent. If you don't know your specific entomology, it would be hard at this stage to match up the pupa with the corresponding larval form.

The same is true of the adult caddisflies: They seldom bear much resemblance to the pupae. At a given and unknown signal, these grubs chew off the ends of their cases and swim to the surface to pop out of their pupal sheaths. This is usually a nearly instantaneous process. Such a burst of speed can be explained by the fact that a pair of their long legs extends outside the sac and acts as a set of powerful oars. Then, too, a large bubble of gas forms at this time inside the pupal sac, which also helps pop them to the surface. Some species can leave their cases and be fully airborne in little more than a second.

This Poseidon-missile zoom to the surface tantalizes the trout, who give chase as if challenged to a race. The surest sign that trout are feeding on emerging caddises, rather than mayflies, is an explosive, slashing rise form followed by the sight of a winged caddisfly zigzagging upwards from the boil. Trout must feel frustrated at missing so many mouthfuls and this seems to fuel their feeding frenzy.

The winged caddisfly adults look much like moths, to which they are closely related. Both have wings covered with tiny scales that render them opaque. Caddises, though, position their wings when at rest differently than moths do. They collapse them in a horizontal inverted V that envelopes their bodies, whereas most moths spread their wings to the side like delta-winged fighter planes.

Although caddises have no tails, they make up for this up front with antennae that are often longer than their bodies. They are extremely agile fliers, given to an erratic, zigzagging flight pattern, and can usually dodge attacks from waxwings, blackbirds, and sample-collecting anglers, though they're hardly a match for the nimble swallows.

Caddisflies are granted a more generous adult life-span than mayflies. Unlike ephemerids, who lose their mouth-parts in the act of hatching, trichopteran caddises can drink water—some can even take in food—so they can live a week or two in their final, winged form.

During this period they hide in the foliage during the day and return to the river each evening, flying up it whether or not they're scheduled for mating and egg-laying at that particular time. This event seems almost social, although it may serve some vital, but hidden, purpose. It certainly can mislead the fly-fisher who, seeing the swarm— sometimes a blizzard—of caddises flying upriver, thinks he's witnessing a superhatch when, in fact, sometimes few, or perhaps none, of the airborne insects may have hatched out that evening.

Still, this overhead armada excites the trout. They hover on the fin, poised to slash at any egg-layer or water-player briefly skipping along the surface, as many caddises do. These adults present difficult targets, however, and the trout seem to miss as many as they catch.

When caddisflies are aloft or afloat, it pays to alter your fishing tactics drastically. In all the dry-fly incidents I've described up to this point I was using the classic, basically upstream presentation to make my fly drift back downcurrent in the exact path an unattached, natural insect would follow. However, that is not an effective way to fish a downwinged floater when trout are slashing at caddises.

The dark blue caddis, which emerges throughout the entire month of June, is perhaps my favorite hatch on the Neversink. The action often lasts only an hour or less, which is a short time frame, but it can be a rewarding one. This crowding of the taking-time into the period just before darkness usually limits me to four or five possible catches on even the best of nights, but there's a consolation for this. The size of the fish I take during this hatch averages far larger than at any other time of the year. It has occurred to me that perhaps it takes larger, and therefore faster, trout to even enter the sudden, caddis-catching game.

The drill I've found most effective is to cast across and slightly downstream to a seen or suspected fish, rather than in the usual upstream direction. I also try to throw a distinct, downcurrent curve in line and leader, which is easy enough to accomplish if I slant my rod in a diagonal plane. Then, within a second after the fly hits the water, I sharply flick up my rod tip a few inches so that it will just rock or barely twitch the imitation. I then let it float as far as it will without seriously dragging.

The rationale behind this oddball delivery is that caddises are extremely active when they find themselves on the water surface—whether hatching out, buzzing the water, or actually laying eggs—and they always kick and struggle in an upcurrent direction. The across-and-downstream delivery insures that when I twitch my down-wing imitation on the surface, it will lurch in a convincing, upstream direction.

There are endless minor variations of this technique, of course, but nine times out of ten you have to add this distinctive motion to your presentation to convince a decent trout. Just presenting an accurate facsimile of the natural doesn't cut it when these flies are on the water. You have to throw in an imitation of their behavior as well.

In this type of fishing I use a sensibly stout leader-tippet: Four-pound-test is minimum and I feel more comfortable with five. Since the fly reaches the fish first, and the leader is pointing away from the trout, ultrafineness isn't critical. When a trout wallops my imitation, he'll be striking against an almost straight line, so even with a strong leader I keep my rod tip up a bit to help cushion the shock.

If, as many claim, the take is the climax of any fly-fishing experience, this explosive, water-scattering burst to a twitched caddis has to be that triumphant moment redoubled in no-trump. I will never cease to be amazed that a half-inch insect can incite an act of such murderous intensity.

Less abundant than caddisflies and mayflies, but still an important food source, are the Plecoptera, or stoneflies—so-named because most live under stones or flat rocks. They fill a crucial niche in the trouts' annual food requirement because they're the most available insects in winter and early spring. Many species start hatching out on clement days as early as February, two months or more before the first mayflies can be expected. Then, too, some species are enormous—nearly as large as your little finger—and it takes only one of these to fill the stomach of the average-sized trout.

All stoneflies, regardless of size, are easy to identify because all species are surprisingly alike in shape and proportions. All larvae have tubular bodies—they're never flattened as most mayflies are—, two short, sturdy tails, and two prominent antennae. They also have two distinct sets of wing pads, while mayflies appear to have only one.

Adult stoneflies are clumsy fliers, churning along like helicopters, and their four wings of equal size are clearly visible and separate, while mayflies appear to have only one pair. At rest, stoneflies fold their translucent wings, which are only slightly longer than their bodies, in a flat plane along the tops of their backs rather than in the inverted, abdomen-enveloping V of caddises.

All stoneflies have a simple, two-stage life cycle. After hatching out into tiny larvae, they feed, grow, and moult several times (as mayflies do) to grow larger exoskeletons. Most hatch out after one year, but a few of the giant species take two or even three years to attain maturity. When fully grown, they make an underwater march to the shoreline, crawl out on the marginal rocks, split open their larval cases, and spread their rapidly growing wings.

This may sound like a trout-proof exercise for stoneflies, but that is not actually the case. During their shoreward crawl they are extremely vulnerable to the alert trout. And since they usually take several minutes to dry their wings before takeoff, many get blown out onto the water surface by gusts of wind before they're able to fly.

They're especially vulnerable to fish during egg-laying because most species of stoneflies alight on the water while ovipositing. Then too, once this essential act is finished, the dead and dying insects present helpless targets.

The rather large inventory of mayflies, caddisflies, and stoneflies may appear to present the trout with all they can eat all the time. But the feasts are only occasional ones because most nymphs and larvae, no matter how abundant, spend the majority of their lives hiding under stones, safe from the trout.

In fact, if it weren't for other available food items, trout couldn't eke out a living. Some trout are too small, others too large, to prosper on a diet of medium-sized insects alone. Even the aquatic-insect eaters need between-meal snacks. Fortunately, for fish of all sizes the stream has other resources that fill in the food gaps.

12

Side Orders

The other types of insects that spend portions of their lives in the riverbed are too numerous to list here, but there are many, ranging from the infamous, bloodsucking blackflies to predatory, four-inch dragonflies. Trout eat their fair share of these insects, though their numbers don't compare with the swarms provided by the big-three aquatics.

Of little importance to fly-fishers, but crucial to the fishery, are the tiny midges of the order Diptera. Only when the sunlight strikes the water at a special angle does one really notice the clouds of these flies that hover above the water all season long. Medium-sized trout rarely bother with the mite-sized insects, but the subyearlings—fish under five inches—owe their lives to them. They not only dine on the underwater larvae, but they pick off the thousands of winged adults that die of old age each day and drop to the surface of the river.

In fact, the supply of these insects is so bountiful that the river teems with young-of-the-year trout. It's the larger mayflies, stoneflies, and caddises that the Neversink needs more of.

Catchable-size trout do get extra rations to supplement their basic diet of aquatics from a wide variety of insects whose relationship to the river is purely accidental. A certain percentage of all small creatures that wiggle, walk, or fly end up in the river inadvertently. Studies have shown that on some rivers up to 40 percent of all trout food in July and August is made up of insects that had no intention of going near the water, but ended up in the drink through clumsiness or sheer bad luck.

The most numerous of these are ants and beetles. In some areas there are springtime infestations of caterpillars and green inchworms, but I have never seen significant numbers of either in our valley. Grasshoppers and small leafhoppers can also be big factors in meadow country, though not on the Neversink where trees line the banks for 99 percent of its length.

I do find some black, three-quarter-inch ground beetles in early-season trout, but only occasionally and usually only one to the customer, so I don't find them worth imitating. Ants are another matter, though.

We are loaded with ants, probably hundred of species, ranging from the nearly inch-long black carpenter ants that scare me into periodic inspections of my house's timbers, down to some tiny gingers that crowd invisibility. While any or all of these may crawl or fall into the river and be eaten, there is only one species I can count on to produce rising trout several days each season.

Starting in mid-August and running until mid-September, on sunny, hot, still afternoons I look for clouds of honey-colored, size 16 flying ants—but *only* on those afternoons when all three of these requirements have been met. Sunny and hot are common conditions at that time of year, but if it is windy or even breezy, as it often is during clear, high-pressure weather, the ants remain grounded.

These ants nearly always appear about three o'clock in the afternoon—never in the morning—and vanish quickly about two hours later when temperatures start to drop. Over the years, I have learned to rely on the weather more and my eyesight less because a flight can be quite local, or at least patchy, and if I don't happen to be in the right place I may not witness the event.

For some reason, water holds a fatal attraction for these insects. They always fly to the river, then up and down it—many actually landing on it. This is a terminal act because once in the surface film, ants are trapped for the rest of their brief lives. Trout seem aware of their helplessness and lie in the slow water, rocking up in a leisurely manner to sip in their victims.

The year before last was the best ant season within memory, providing a total of five flying-ant-fishing days, and the very last day of August was the best one of the bunch. It was a warm, sunny day and the air was so still that a slight haze developed. After lunch I started glassing the pool just below my house with binoculars every half hour, looking for the telltale rings of rising fish.

By 3:30 P.M. the water was still quiet, but I suited up and headed downriver anyway. Even though I hadn't seen a single ant in the air, conditions were so perfect I felt there had to be a swarming nearby. I waited and watched patiently by a slow-water stretch and tied on my favorite imitation. This is a wasp-waisted pattern with two separate egg-shaped body-sections of dark cinnamon with a bunch of dun hackle fibers tied flat along the back. On a light-wire No. 16 hook, it barely floats—just like a trapped ant.

It was nearly four-thirty and I was about to give up when I saw the first rise, which was quickly followed by another. I was creeping into position to cover these two risers when it seemed that the whole pool became covered with circles and I began seeing ant bodies drifting past my boots.

For the next two hours I enjoyed the classic dry-fly fishing that Brits who fish their southern chalk streams have written so glowingly about. Fish rose so regularly that I could observe individual fish carefully and pick out only the better ones. I have the impression that trout relish ants even more than their staple mayflies, and when they're gorging on this rare feast they'll take a good imitation with greater confidence than at any other time.

Exactly how many trout I took that day my diary doesn't tell because I had to admit in the day's write-up that I had lost all count. It was certainly well over thirty, though, and all from two places—the improved flat and the pool just below my house. There were no big fish, however. Most were brook trout, and three browns of about twelve inches were the best of the day. It has been my experience that despite this sudden glut of food, the biggest fish are reluctant to come out of hiding in low, clear water when the light is that bright.

It wasn't until the next day that I solved the mystery of that great, invisible flight. People around Claryville and just below said there were yellow clouds of ants buzzing around for nearly two hours that afternoon. The only ones I ever saw two miles downriver were the dead and dying ones that had taken over an hour to raft their way downstream.

The largest trout in the stream show little interest in insects of any kind or size. Some innate wisdom warns them that expending several calories of energy to capture back only a fraction of one is a mug's game. They set their sights on bigger prey, which the river also provides. A three- to four-inch minnow contains more protein and calories than dozens of mayflies and can usually be captured with one well-executed swoop. Because of this dietary preference, the oversized trout that often dominate large, deep pools are usually referred to as "old cannibals," but this label appears to be an exaggeration.

During the years when I was a mighty killer of trout, I scrupulously examined the stomach contents of all my victims. The most common minnows found there were the mottled-brown sculpins and darters that hide, stationary, on the stream bottom. This seemed logical because a sitting duck is an easier target than a speeding one. Well over 90 percent of all the minnows or their remains that I found were from these two relatively similar species. Even partly digested corpses could be readily identified by their wide, flattened skulls.

I found only an occasional black-nosed dace in the stomachs. In the lower river these small fish easily outnumber sculpins and darters combined, yet they're relatively agile and are seldom caught by trout.

I also discovered that the eating of other fishes wasn't the exclusive habit of large trout. I have found minnows in the stomachs of two-year-old brook and brown trout—fish in the seven- to nine-inch category. This is not a regular occurrence, but apparently, when an easy target presents itself, relatively small trout appreciate the fish course, too.

For the record, I found only one identifiable small trout in all the stomachs I examined. So, while large trout are admittedly piscivorous, the term "cannibal" is probably a bum rap. The rare occurrence of trout dining out on their own kin is probably not due to ethical or moral scruples, though. It's just that small trout are by far the fastest, most nimble fish in the river, so fewer are chased and even fewer captured.

There's one other source of big-fish food in the Neversink that often goes unnoticed. Crawfish, being nocturnal roamers, are seldom seen but are reasonably plentiful, and undigested claw shells appear frequently in the mush of stomach contents. Only when I started rearranging underwater rocks did I become aware of how many of these crustaceans the river supported. They are members of a relatively small—three inches long is a big one—unmarketable species. Still, that makes a decent lobster cocktail, even for a trout of several pounds.

Most slow-moving, weedy trout streams produce an abundance of freshwater shrimps and scuds, or sow bugs, but these food sources are rare to nonexistent in slightly acidic freestone waters. I have found a few sow bugs in still-water holes that have been scoured out by past floods and lie adjacent to the river, but I have never come across one in a river trout's stomach. It's a pity we don't have them because where they're numerous they're said to build plump, red-fleshed trout.

This inventory of trout food is undoubtedly similar to the variety offered by other Catskill rivers, but the quantities in the Neversink were skimpier. I could think of no other explanation for the fact that our trout were both fewer and generally smaller.

To remedy this, I turned to giving free handouts. One obvious source of natural trout food was the underutilized dace. A tubular, wire-mesh minnow trap, baited with bread crusts and moored in a slow-water deep, usually lured a couple of dozen at each setting. These I would dump into a half-filled coffee can and transport to a spot several feet upcurrent of a cribbing.

However, I couldn't just toss them in and expect the trout to clean them up. After all, there were plenty of dace milling around nearby, completely unmolested. The trick was, I discovered after some experimenting, to pinch them firmly with a thumbnail just ahead of their tails, dislocating a vertebra or two. Then, when plopped in, they swam feebly and erratically as they drifted downcurrent, and nine times out of ten a good trout would shoot out from under the cribbing and nail the handicapped minnow. Apparently, trout are as merciless as I am.

Another ready food source was the plague of Japanese beetles that raided my raspberry patch each summer, turning leaves into green lace doilies. These too were harvested into a coffee can and trickled as a living chum-line over known trout lies. Fish relish beetles and very few struggled for long in the entrapping surface film.

All this created a good show—the kids loved to watch the trout feed—but it was a time-consuming exercise and, I had to admit, wasn't adding up to much. The Japanese beetle infestation lasts only a few weeks, and it was a bumper harvest when I could trap and deliver a pound of dace during an entire weekend.

The smart play, I felt, would be to use my time to make improvements farther down the food chain, concentrating on those that might be long-lasting. One obvious idea was to try to increase the living quarters for aquatic insects as I had done for the trout.

During all my rock-moving, I had discovered that flat rock slabs—ones shaped roughly like giant slates—harbored far more insects per square foot of river bottom than rounded ones did. Their undersides, lying on uneven cobbles, were bathed with a constant flow of water and offered sanctuary for vulnerable nymphs and larvae. The bottoms of rounded stones, on the other hand, were usually cemented into the riverbed, and only a small ring just above its disappearance underground offered likely insect lodgings.

On a downriver reconnaissance I discovered along the right bank two sections of cliff that looked unstable and about to collapse. Our local rock formation is sedimentary, a bluestone shale, showing clear lines of layering. Apparently, in these two places, spring trickles had seeped into the horizontal clefts, frozen in wintertime, and separated the rock into large slabs about two inches thick and stacked on top of each other.

I lugged a wrecking bar and a larger crowbar down to the site and, taking care to stand to one side of the expected avalanche, started prying at the tilted slabs. There was, fortunately, no thundering collapse, and by working down from the top layer I could pry out the flat pieces of rock by ones and twos.

Most were well over two- to nearly four-feet across and too heavy to lift, but they could be tilted on edge and then cartwheeled out into the river. After I had quarried all I could from both sites, I bound myself to a solid promise: Every time I passed the site to fish, I would lay down my fly rod, roll a slab out into the nearby riffle, and carefully seat it into a stable lie.

The supply lasted me all that season and well into the next. After the first fall flood receded, I waded downriver to check on my handiwork. I was pleasantly surprised to find that though the high water had altered some parts of the riffle, nearly all my slabs were exactly where I'd placed them, and none were missing. Apparently, the thin leading edge that faced upstream gave the powerful currents little leverage on their relatively large mass, and they were about as floodproof as any movable river rock can be.

I looked forward to Beaver Kill–sized hatches of insects coming into the pool below for the coming season, but that was not to be. Though there was a distinct improvement in fly life, I'd have to rate the increase at about 25 percent. The stinginess of this gain saved me a lot of money, though. If the results had been sensational, I'm sure I'd have tried to pave the entire riverbed with truckfuls of rock slabs carted in at considerable expense. And then, as luck would have it, a hundred-year flood would strike the very next year, bury my slabs under tons of rubble sluiced down from my neighbor's water above, and both the river and I would be poorer again.

Still, I wasn't totally discouraged. It had occurred to me that the insect deficiency might be due to a problem one link farther down the food chain. And that meant back to the books again to find out whether or not the stream-bred insects that trout fed on were, themselves, getting enough to eat.

13

Food of the Food

I suppose that if you follow a stream's food chain back far enough you'll end up at the sun. After all, the simple forms of vegetable life that most aquatic insects feed on may draw their nutrients from the water that bathes them, but they are fueled by solar energy. So between the sun and an aquatic insect on the river bottom, there was a huge area to explore and, perhaps, to tinker with.

The idea of enhancing the lower, more basic links of the food chain rather than the uppermost one through hatchery stocking was in no way original or novel. During my readings on biological research and river husbandry, I'd learned about many such attempts and even a few successes.

One of these was, of course, Frank Sawyer's applications of powdered limestone on the Hampshire Avon. It had dramatically increased insect and other animal life on that docile river and more than paid for itself in added food production. However, such dressings were out of the question on the volatile Neversink.

Another method of applying limestone had attracted attention back in the 1930s. A small West Virginia creek that had become lethally acidic due to coal-mine tailings had been restored to trout productivity by an ingenious and continuous dispenser. Chunks of limestone rock were placed inside a huge, sturdy barrel that had been fitted with vanes. It was then mounted on an axle, like a waterwheel, where the stream flow would rotate it. The rocks, grinding against each other as they tumbled inside, metered out a constant supply of lime particles into the stream water, neutralizing the acidity.

This must have been an extremely gentle, flood-free body of water. Any actuary who'd even quote a premium of any price to insure such a Rube Goldberg machine in the Neversink would be hauled away in a straitjacket.

I then dreamed up a third, though perhaps not original, way of dispensing lime—one that was virtually flood-proof and should pay for itself since it offered real economic, as well as fishery, benefits. What if all the pastures and hay meadows up and down the Valley were spread with lime each spring? Such dressings would grow lusher crops and grass and the carbonates would leach into the river on a steady basis.

When I suggested this to the cattleman who grazed a couple dozen head of Social-Register cattle on a Valley farm, he just laughed. "I tried that on one of my pastures a few years ago. There's a bed of small cobblestones just under this thin layer of topsoil. The first good rain flushed that lime right on through. I tested that soil six weeks later and it was just as acid as it was before I started."

So, the good news was that the high-pH drainage water would reach the river even faster and with greater efficiency than I'd thought. The bad news was that no farmer in his right mind was going to spread any agricultural lime at all.

Streambed vegetation, usually called waterweed, is a great asset to a river, and the fisheries, mainly chalk streams and spring creeks, that have the most abundant insect hatches are usually paved with it. There are two good reasons why weeds—especially the dense, beneficial ones—encourage aquatic insects. First, they increase the area of pasture. A fist-sized rock may have four or five square inches of algae-covered surface for insects to nibble on, but a clump of weed with its many leaves and stems can offer several times that amount of surface for algae colonization. Second, and far more important, a dense clump of vegetation offers vital concealment for hundreds of nymphs and larvae, while the small stone provides little in the way of sanctuary.

River keepers on the best-maintained British fisheries spend so much time and effort looking after waterweeds that they might better be called river farmers. They yank out by the roots the strong, stringy varieties, which offer little insect cover and often break fly-fishers' leaders, so that the denser, low-lying ones can take over that area. And in midsummer when weeds—even the beneficial ones—start choking the river flow, river keepers mow large patches and channels through the growth to clear out areas for fly-fishing.

I have tried to establish many types of weeds in the Neversink, transplanting the ones teeming with scuds and insects that I'd found in the gentle, compensation flows of our river below the dam. Some didn't appreciate the new neighborhood and quickly disappeared. The few that looked like they were going to make it were ripped out by the first high water, even though I'd ballasted their roots under the edges of large, flat rocks.

Biologists have since told me that, if a stream environment is congenial to a certain species of weed, it will already be there. Apparently, wading birds bring in enough seeds and cuttings from nearby waters to effect transplanting. When the streambed, gradient, velocity, and water chemistry aren't to its liking, no amount of transplanting can establish a waterweed. Here endeth the lesson.

One of the few wild geese I haven't chased is the transplanting of new species of aquatic insects. Early on, I'd been forewarned by one of Hewitt's books, which told of his attempts to establish the large mayfly called the Green Drake in the Neversink. He'd gone to a richer, nearby river where they abounded, caught many egg-laying females with a butterfly net, and rushed their egg cases back to the Neversink in a pail of water. He reported only token hatches that dwindled to nothing in a few years. Again the biologists say that, like waterweeds, insects will transplant themselves from other waters only if conditions in a river change to meet their requirements.

One apparently successful stream-enrichment substance I'd never even consider is sugar. A few years back, some biologists working for a state fish and game department metered a solution of sucrose into a controlled-flow section of stream and reported that this produced several times as many aquatic insects as in the untreated section just above. Why they chose sucrose—a simple sugar that isn't a factor in natural stream water—I'll never know. Were funds for the project supplied by Domino Sugar?

There is, however, one natural additive that does grow bigger salmonids faster. Many modern hatcheries add liquid oxygen to the water supply for their rearing tanks and claim that the extra poundage of trout and salmon this produces more than pays for the lox and metering equipment. I have no doubt that this is efficient in a closed hatchery system, but I can't believe it would be practical with the volume and length of a sizable river system.

So, after all my research, reading, and failed or rejected experiments, my attention turned back to the algae which most aquatic insects dine on exclusively. Even the few predatory species depend on algae because they live off smaller algae-eaters.

These minute vegetable organisms are the lowest living link in a river's food chain. Though some biologists believe that algae can't colonize underwater surfaces until those have been presettled by bacteria, the latter are apparently so omnipresent in all water, fresh or salt, still or running, that the issue is theoretical rather than functional.

Algae coat all underwater surfaces with a thin film like a pale, brownish slime. They're the cause of 99 percent of a wader's spills and dunkings. They're also the reason why streams can support so many kinds and numbers of aquatic insects.

Fortunately, algae are an incredibly abundant and rapidly renewable resource. My studies of poachers' boot tracks had taught me that these organisms will recoat a scraped rock in as little as five days during warm, sunny weather, and within two weeks even in midwinter. I have yet to find a single rock in the Neversink—or in any other river, for that matter—that had been nibbled down to its abrasive surface by aquatic insects. They simply can't keep up with this seemingly endless supply of fodder.

Obviously, our stingy supply of aquatic insects couldn't be blamed on lack of food. There were other ominous possibilities, though. Possibly a lack of available carbonates in the slightly acidic river water limited the insects' essential process of building exoskeletons—though I hoped this wasn't a major cause because I'd long ago sworn off limestone. Most probably the shortage was due to a lack of adequate living quarters.

One other, though less important, source of insect food was worth looking into: the vegetable detritus that drops or is blown into the stream. Some insects, mainly caddisflies, live off the dead leaves and small twigs that end up in the water. Leaves floating freely downriver can't be considered part of this food source because snail-paced caddises can't possibly chase or catch them, and those leaves that collect in backwaters and eddies aren't much better because they're easily flushed away by a modest high water. Only those immobilized by being wedged under rocks or crammed into interstices can be counted as available food. As a result, the structure of the river bottom dictates the amount of leaf food that can be collected and utilized. Streambeds made up of rounded boulders and cannonball-shaped rocks trap very little. Slab rocks, especially those resting on an uneven bed, allowing water to flow under as well as over them, collect the most. Jumbles of angular rocks are the next best collecting areas.

Only a few sections on my water, namely those directly below cliffs or precipitous hillsides, were blessed with rocks having anything like those kinds of leave-collecting bottoms. Most of my stretch, and indeed, most of the entire river, was paved with rounded cobbles that probably had once been jagged-edged rocks. But over the years—possibly centuries—they had been rounded by downriver tumbling and further smoothed by abrasive sand transported by floodwaters. Clearly, this offered only marginal terrain for trapping organic debris and for providing safe-houses for aquatic insects.

There was further evidence that rounded, easily-moved rocks offered insecure lodgings for insects. After a few years on the river, I could predict fairly accurately the density of insect hatches for the coming season by the magnitude of the spring flooding. If major portions of the streambed had been altered by the digging or deposition of rocks and gravel, fly hatches would invariably be sparse. If, on the rare other hand, the river was spared serious resculpturing, the number of aquatics would be relatively plentiful. There seemed to be no question but that the tumbling of rocks either crushed insect larvae or left them to the mercy of currents that would sweep them into adjacent fields and woodlots to be stranded by receding waters.

Rebuilding the stream bottom had already been ruled out as both risky and prohibitively expensive. When I could find them, I could wheel large flat rocks out into the riverbed and pry up existing ones, but this was tokenism. My efforts to improve the river at a fundamental level had run into a solid stone wall made up of rounded cobbles.

Frustrated by this blockage, I began to envy a Connecticut multi-millionaire I'd recently heard about. He'd bought a vast estate within commuting distance of New York City, but felt underprivileged because there wasn't a trout stream or even any running water on his property, so he decided he'd build himself one, starting from scratch.

First he had a curving channel excavated on a long stretch of hillside. Then he had rocks of specified sizes and shapes trucked in and carefully positioned in the dry bed to form a series of runs and pools with appropriate interstices for insects and overhead cover for trout. Voilà, an instant trout stream—all you add is water.

Wells were drilled to supply this and nutrients and minerals had to be added to it for maximum fertility. Trout were then stocked, as well as cadres of various nymphs and larvae. Finally, pumps were installed at the bottommost collecting pool and all the water was returned through pipes to the top of the stream—during which trip it was refrigerated in summer and heated in winter. The end result was a three-hundred-yard-long, twenty-five-foot-wide ersatz trout stream that operated on the principle of an escalator.

Don't for a moment think I'm creative enough to have dreamed this one up. An utterly reliable friend of mine reported it to me after he'd just been given a personal, guided tour by the proud creator.

I've been accused of trying to make our river run uphill, but even I can't imagine playing God on such a vast scale, even if money were no object. It would probably be cheaper and more rewarding to buy several miles of super spring creek and a private jet to commute to it. Still, the man had pointed the way: If it was possible to create a near-perfect trout stream out of a bare hillside, merely improving an existing good one should be child's play.

Whether or not this would prove to be true, it gave me new incentives. But by now I realized I had been looking for utopia in the wrong direction. To find a practical way to improve my fishery, I was going to have to backtrack up the path I'd been taking and start looking for a solution I'd overlooked farther up the food chain.

14

"Let there be lights . . ."

Since it appeared to be beyond my powers to significantly increase the supply of stream-bred insects, I started looking for a parallel, or supplementary, food source. The solution seemed obvious, but the obvious wasn't the solution.

For decades, hatcheries have been raising trout on artificial pellets, and the latest versions of these small, dry cylinders are said to provide the perfect mix of a trout's nutritional requirements. I wouldn't think of challenging the biologists' analysis of the ideal trout diet nor their ability to recreate it. The only problem I have with their product is that I can't get wild trout to eat it.

Over the years, I'd tossed enough pellets into the river to risk tennis elbow, and yet my fish would not feed on them. Only once did I see one of my trout take a pellet into his mouth—and he spat it out instantly. Apparently, a wild trout's gums don't find hard, unyielding objects anything like squishy insect bodies, and pellets probably flunk the taste test as well. There's no point in yelling "Eat—it will make you big and strong when you grow up." Trout are even less persuadable than small children.

I must admit I have seen wild trout take pellets, but only under special circumstances. I've watched a caretaker feed a heavily stocked stretch of the Neversink, and all the domestic fish pounced on the pellets as if it were feeding time back at the hatchery. Once they'd been boiling regularly for a few minutes, I saw a few wild trout join in. It seems that feeding activity among trout is as social and contagious as it is among chickens. However, loading up my water with large, stocked shills seemed a self-defeating way to cram more food into native trout.

Some time after my inadequate feeding attempts with dace and Japanese beetles, I did hit upon a method of supplying natural insect food that actually dispensed itself and really worked. Well, almost.

Before I sank my garden fence two feet underground, woodchucks kept tunneling under the wire while I was away during the week. As soon as my .22 claimed one, another seemed to show up. To avoid a total loss from these depredations, I decided to convert my romaine and broccoli into nutritious trout food.

I'd read somewhere that British poachers used to hang a sheep's head, or the like, from a tree over a trout pool; when the dropping maggots had attracted a cluster of trout, the fish were easy marks for a maggot impaled on a small hook. Guessing that a plump woodchuck was as good as or better than a gristly sheep's head, I strung up my victims from tree limbs overhanging one of my lower, deeper pools.

In a few days, a steady supply of maggots began trickling out of the carcasses—especially during the heat of the day. A school of trout assembled below each one, and I could almost see them putting on heft with each passing day. This feeding system offered natural food, was fully automated, kept on dispensing while I was away in the city, and was, I felt, the ultimate solution. Then one hot day my wife and kids dropped down to the pool for a swim. As they ran back to the house shrieking and holding their noses, I knew that was the end of an inspired fishery-improvement scheme.

Casting about for another handy source of trout food, I dimly remembered reading in a book by Ed Hewitt (yes, there's that man again) that the best supplemental trout food was ground-up lungs, or lights. He claimed that, while perhaps not as rich a diet as the chopped liver that hatcheries fed in his day, lights were superior river food for two reasons. First, since lung tissue is made up of tiny air sacs that make it float, it trains trout to look for their food on the surface, which is what every fly-fisher wants. Second, floating food has little or no waste. Chopped liver quickly sinks to the bottom and is lost in rock interstices, whereas the floating lights that weren't eaten in the first pool bobbed on downcurrent to be cleaned up by the trout below.

While the great man had the reputation of being always positive and sometimes right, this seemed too good a lead to pass up. I went to my local butcher and asked for twenty pounds of lungs. After convincing him that I was serious, he told me that only a few shops in heavily German neighborhoods ever carried them and that a slaughter-house was my best bet.

After some research I finally located a small, nearby abatoir that slaughtered and halved veal for wholesalers. The head man seemed willing enough to sell me whole lungs at the going rate (pet-food canners purchase seldom-eaten spare parts in bulk), but explained that he would have to discolor them first with charcoal dust. Apparently, this procedure had been enacted into state law to prevent unscrupulous retailers from adulterating their hamburger with a cheap substitute. It took me a half hour to convince him that I wasn't a crooked butcher, merely a harmless eccentric who had a crush on trout.

After I'd cut away the cartilaginous tracheae, I lugged the lungs down to my local butcher, who'd agreed to run the lot through his grinder for a fee if I appeared at closing time, when he had to clean the machine anyway. The resulting lungburger was stuffed into plastic bags in five-pound lots and parked in my freezer for future use.

It had been quite an exercise, but it turned out to have been worth it. The very first time I ladled out a couple of pounds into a riffle above a good pool I was rewarded by the sight of dozens of fish swirling and splashing down in the slow water. This show was as humbling as it was gratifying because I'd never been able to raise anything like that number of trout when fishing my way up the pool.

Hewitt had been 101 percent right, after all. Here was a relatively cheap food in endless supply that even wild trout would gorge on. These tiny blobs of meat may not present the silhouette of any known insect, but trout wallop them the first time they see them. Apparently, the smell of lights, or of the blood that trickles out of them, identifies them instantly as lean red meat. Our gentle, shy trout seem to have the noses and appetites of piranhas.

The two- to three-pound dosage I usually mete out during a feeding may not sound like much, but when the particles separate in the turbulence of a pool's inflow currents, they number in the many thousands. After ten or so handfuls have been scattered, they'll cover a pool fifty feet wide and two hundred feet long with over a dozen red specks per square foot of surface, creating an artificial red tide. I have never, at any time on any river, seen that many natural insects floating down a pool.

This synthetic super-hatch usually lasts only two or three minutes, but the trout, brookies in particular, make the most of it. Some will hold just under the surface and grab the overhead particles with a rapid, rocking-horse motion. A few gluttons will eat their way steadily up the pool until they're within a few feet of me and, when the food supply peters out, charge down to the tail and start gulping their way up again with their dorsal fins cutting the surface.

Such performances go a long way toward explaining the surprising mobility of pool-dwelling trout. They may be bunched up in the deep fast water at the head of the pool all day only to drift down to the tail end at dusk for easier feeding on dead or dying insects. Apparently, this migration can take place extremely quickly when a food source sends out the right signals.

Trout living in fast runs and pockets will nail these meat particles readily enough as they speed by, but they rarely follow the food stream down into the slow flat or pool below. It seems that homesteading and defending the choice lie they've won is higher on their list of priorities than a few extra mouthfuls of food.

The largest fish in a pool, almost always brown trout, seldom wallow on the surface, but they, too, get their share. About ten percent of the lungburger sinks slowly because its air sacs have been ruptured in grinding and, as a result, becomes easy pickings for bigger, more cautious fish. When the light is right, I can make out the golden flashes from their sides as they twist and turn to intercept the red blobs drifting just above the streambed.

Feeding trout this way is almost as much fun as fishing. There may be an element of playing God to it since trout appear and perform at my bidding, but that's not the major attraction. What fascinates most is the insight this gives into where trout live and how and when they feed.

Through supplemental feeding I have located trout lies in places I never suspected. Some will settle in surprisingly shallow water and well away from the current as long as there's the overriding amenity of overhead cover. Spotting trout this way seems to me a form of cheating. After all, trout have a right to some privacy, too. However, the greater good of the extra food squelches my misgivings about such prying.

The most exciting and revealing trout feeding requires an accomplice. I like to position myself one-third to halfway down a pool, preferably ten to fifteen feet up a steep bank, while a volunteer stands in the run above with bucket in hand. When I say, "Okay, let her go," dispensing begins and soon the trout start feeding, at first hesitantly and then with abandon. From this perspective, I can tell not only the size but also the species of the feeders, both of which are impossible from upriver. Many of my sightings are of fish I've never raised, or even suspected the existence of, in that section of stream.

One trout secret that still eludes me is where these fish hide when they're not on the feed. From my perch on the hillside I can scrutinize the stream bottom of at least one-third of the pool, and I can usually make out only three or four small trout hovering just above the rocks. Then, when the lungburger blankets the surface, a dozen or two will appear out of nowhere. Try as I will, I can't catch these fish emerging from their hides or returning to them, nor can I count enough large, undercut rocks on the bottom to house them all. A trip through the area in a wet suit with mask and snorkel doesn't turn up the fish or their sanctuaries, either.

The most valuable lesson I've learned from this feeding and spying is when—or, more accurately, under which conditions—trout will feed greedily and when they'll abstain. If I scatter lights at a poor time or under adverse conditions only two or three small fish will respond, rising only once or twice each. On the other hand, at the best of times, the same dosage in the same pool will induce forty to fifty trout to feed voraciously for several minutes. The contrast is astonishing.

After years of feeding, I can now predict with 99 percent accuracy how trout will respond to my handouts long before I reach the feeding area. All I need to do is check the cloud cover and river level and reconfirm what they tell me with a stream thermometer.

If the water level is up half a foot or more due to a recent rain, feeding response will be poor to marginal. I know I'll get the same reaction if the day is, or has been, cloudy, regardless of river height. On the other hand, when the sun is out and the river is at normal flow,

I can look forward to a full show of eager splashers *if* I choose the right time of day. The triggering factors are water temperature and its rate of change, and my thermometer can readily pinpoint the best feeding time, or times, for the day.

All this is not nearly as mysterious as it may sound. Trout feeding activity is dictated by their metabolism rate and this, in turn, is a function of body temperature. Since trout are cold-blooded creatures, their bodies are essentially the same temperature as the water they're swimming in. When the river heats up or cools down, they do, too.

Biologists have determined that brown trout metabolism peaks at 63 degrees. The figure may be slightly lower for brook trout and a shade higher for rainbows, but 63 degrees is close enough for our purposes. At that reading, a trout's gills are most efficient in extracting oxygen from the water, its digestion rate is most rapid, and all bodily functions are performing at top efficiency.

Obviously, then, trout feeding should be most active when water temperature is nearest to the magic number 63—and it almost always is. But there's a joker in the deck. A flat, unchanging 63 degrees always means that lights-feeding and fly-fishing will be only mediocre at best. It is only when the rate of change toward and through 63 degrees is rapid that fish will feed like gluttons.

You get these rapid changes only in fair weather when the sun's rays warm up stream-bottom rocks, which then transmit this heat to the water flowing over them. The lower and slower the water, and the more hours of sunshine, the faster the heat-up. Similarly, in late afternoon and evening, heat will radiate out of both rocks and stream water fastest when clear skies abet this escape.

During sunny, high-pressure weather in July, the spread of temperatures I record on the lower Neversink may surprise you. At daybreak after a clear night during average flows I usually get 54 degrees. By 11:00 A.M. it will be up to 60 degrees, by noon 62 degrees, and by 1:00 P.M., 64 degrees. Temperature will continue to climb until 4:30 or

5:00 P.M. when it will peak at about 70 degrees. After that, readings start to drop off and should be down to 64 or 65 degrees just before dark. There has been a variation of 16 degrees during that eighteen-hour period, and I can expect active feeding to take place only from 11:00 A.M. to 1:00 P.M. and from 8:00 P.M. until dark.

If the day is cloudy after a cloudy night, on the other hand, temperature variation will be minimum: 60 degrees at 8:00 A.M., 61 degrees at noon, 63 degrees at 4:00 P.M., and 62 degrees at dusk. Trout may take an occasional mouthful of food at any time during that period, but at no time will they feed voraciously.

Why doesn't a flat 63 degrees produce aggressive feeding all day long? I'm convinced that the reason for this is that the supply of oxygen in the trout's bloodstream, though high, remains constant when temperatures are stable. On the other hand, when temperatures are racing up or down toward and through the magic 63 mark, trout are getting a sudden surge of oxygen through rapidly increasing gill efficiency. Whether or not this gives the fish the "high" that we experience when we hyperventilate though forced breathing, I have no clue. I only know from years of observation that fly-fishing success and active feeding on lights are both at their peak under these rapid-change conditions. I have written in a previous book a lengthy documentation with complex charts explaining how and why this works so I won't bore you with the complicated calculations here. Just take my word for it: When temperatures race through the lower to mid-sixties from either direction, trout will feed with a near frenzy, and they simply never do when the thermometer stalls at that mark.

Having discovered this, I could then both fish and feed with far greater efficiency than before. In sunny, summer weather, I'd hit the stream with rod and lights bucket at 11:00 A.M. Leaving the food at the head of a pool, I'd walk down to the tail and fish my way back up. When I'd covered the water to my satisfaction, I'd distribute half the lungburger, saving the rest for the pool above, which would receive the identical treatment. Evenings, I'd go out at 8:00 P.M. and follow the same procedure on a different stretch.

I couldn't resist showing off my fish-feeding prowess to the other fly-fishers in the Valley and they were duly impressed with the spectacle my fish put on. One donated an old but working freezer, which we installed in an empty shed behind the general store. I kept it stocked with bags of frozen lights and the other users put a check mark beside their names every time they picked up a bag. All accounts were settled at the end of the season.

This program, I felt, was nearly ideal. Fish were getting extra rations all up and down the Valley rather than just in my limited stretch. Then too, this feeding was actually cost-efficient. If four pounds of lights would, indeed, build a pound of wild-trout flesh, as biologists said, that quantity of lungs could be bought, ground, and stored at half the price of a pound of inferior hatchery trout. I was convinced that the Neversink would soon regain its position as one of the most productive trout fisheries in the East.

15

". . . and there was lights"

Feeding artificial pellets to trout is as simple as scooping a pailful of cracked corn out of a bin and scattering it around the chicken pen. It's a no-fuss, no-mess operation.

I'm afraid I can't say the same for feeding ground-up lungs. I wasn't aware of any difficulties during my first lights-feeding years because I'd worked the procedure into my daily schedule. While I was making the morning coffee at six-thirty or seven, I'd listen to the weather report on the radio and double-check on river level and cloud cover with a glance out the window. If all seemed propitious, I'd pull a bag of lights out of the freezer in my cellar, put it into a small, plastic pail and lug it upstairs to start thawing while the water dripped through the automatic coffeemaker.

In five hours, or by about eleven o'clock, when I expected to go fishing, all but a central core the size of a softball would be thawed. Half the bag, or some two and a half pounds, would be fed that morning and the remainder would be saved for an evening feeding on another stretch of river. It became a regular part of my daily weekend or vacation routine and I never found the procedure onerous.

For the others involved in the feeding plan, I now realized, the process would be more complicated and take more planning. If they decided to feed that noon, they had to drive to the store to pick up a bag early enough to allow time for thawing. If they waited until the store opened at 9:00 A.M., so they could pick up the newspaper and a quart of milk as well, they'd be limited to the one feeding that evening.

There was an added problem of occasional overnight storage that we all faced. In hot weather, lights will spoil as fast as ungutted trout. They'll keep fairly well outdoors, since overnight temperatures usually drop down into the low or mid-fifties, but don't leave the bucket on your porch or terrace. The Valley is thick with raccoons and they can sniff out meat every time. The next morning you'll find not only that these bandits have eaten their fill, but that they've smeared any excess over a wide area, making the cleanup a major ordeal.

Of course, the best way to store any leftovers is in the refrigerator, but that's not always possible. A lungburger bucket or pail takes up a lot of space in a usually crowded fridge and, on top of this, females of all ages seem to find the stuff repulsive, or at least yucky.

Why this is so, I have no idea. Lights look to me just like ordinary hamburger except that they're paler—pinkish rather than red. I'll admit they feel different to the touch, though. They will stick like epoxy to anything, and the pink blobs have a habit of somehow getting onto your shirt and pants while you're flinging handfuls out into the current. This makes them even more odious to the family's vice president in charge of laundry.

To counteract these minor inconveniences, I posted instructions and hints in large type on the freezer door. I wanted the other lights users to get such enthusiastic reactions from their trout that they'd disregard any negatives. I listed minimum thawing times and best feeding hours. I advised against feeding during bad weather and under high-water conditions in particular.

There appear to be several reasons why high river levels dampen the trouts' response to lights. Part of this may be due to the fact that rains, which cause high waters, flush a lot of extra, competing food into the river. But the main reasons are that the added volume of water dilutes the fish-attracting odor of the lights, and that their increased speed of travel shortens the period of visual stimulation. Then too, when water volume increases, it doesn't heat up or cool down as readily, but tends to conform to the flat, cloudy-day temperature pattern.

Despite handouts missed due to weather or water, I was feeding about a hundred pounds of lights each year on weekends and vacations. If I'd been a regular resident, I could have easily stoked twice that amount into my trout. That first cooperative year, others used up three freezerfuls or about another three hundred pounds. This meant that the river had to be gaining about a hundred pounds of wild trout each year over and above fish that were being stocked—certainly more fish than were being killed, even if you added in a generous estimate of the poachers' take to the riparian owners' modest harvest. We didn't notice the benefits immediately, but we had to be stockpiling the river with more or larger trout.

The next spring I loaded up the freezer again and plugged it in. We had an exceptionally wet May and June that year and were plagued by high river levels until well into July. A few neighbors started feeding again at that time, but I noticed that the names on the check-off list added up to only half the number that had signed up the previous year. By mid-September, there were still two bags left. I pulled the plug and lugged the bags home for storage in my own freezer.

The program was clearly running out of steam. I questioned the few loyalists about their plans for the next season and their response was so lukewarm I knew riverwide lights-feeding was a thing of the past. Apparently, the process involved too much time and trouble. Some backslid to stocking and pellet-feeding. The following season I was once again the sole dispenser of lights in the Valley.

16

Salar Sebago

One late-April afternoon four seasons ago, I decided to fish the reservoir itself, and chose a stretch where a sizable brook flowed into it. I was playing a hunch that the schools of smelt that spawn up this brook after dark would be resting nearby, and so would a lot of hungry predators. After covering two hundred yards of shoreline without a touch, I decided to sweep that area again, only this time farther out by wading up to the top of my chest-waders. This maximum effort meant shedding my fishing vest with attached net so that the fly boxes in the side pockets wouldn't get soaked.

I had worked well down the shore again and was beginning to congeal from the lengthy and near-total immersion when I felt a solid pull and then saw a large swirl. The fish just held there a few seconds, wagging his tail—probably confused at having been brought up short—then took off for deeper water. At the end of that first sprint, he performed a somersault two feet above the surface and I could see he was BIG. When he ran down the shoreline to my right, I backed slowly into the shallows, letting him run off the reel, and, when

I reached knee-deep water, began applying serious pressure. This goaded him into two more jumps, and after a few more zigzagging runs I felt I had taken the starch out of him.

However, to make that agonizing, five-minute trek back to my vest and net would be asking for a lost fish. I spotted a gently inclined patch of gravel about a hundred feet below me and decided to head in that direction and attempt a beaching. When I'd towed the fish down there and started to back up on dry land, he would have none of it. He wasn't as pooped as I'd thought. On my first two attempts, he panicked when he hit the shallows and made short runs, but on my third try I got him on his side and, keeping pressure on him by backing up steadily, used his flappings to swim him five feet up onto dry land.

At my feet lay a bright, male landlocked salmon with a scimitar tail that was so stiff I could carry him by grabbing the wrist of it the way one can with a mature Atlantic. He measured exactly twenty-four inches, and at four pounds, fourteen ounces he was handily the biggest fish of any species I'd ever taken from Neversink waters. It took all my willpower to keep from carting him off to the taxidermist.

While I felt this capture was a milestone of sorts, I couldn't say it was a complete surprise. Landlocked salmon had been successfully introduced into the upper Neversink over a decade earlier.

Back in the mid-1970s, a state fisheries' biologist—the same one who's since settled in the Valley—paid calls on most riparian owners asking if it would be all right for state crews to enter their land to stock landlocked salmon fingerlings in the river. This caused quite a stir because landlocks, with the possible exception of Atlantic salmon, are the most glamorous of freshwater fishes.

A few owners wanted assurances that this wouldn't harm existing trout populations. And everyone wanted to know what sort of salmon fishing we could expect if the program succeeded.

The answer to the first query was that trout and salmon were usually compatible, rather than competitive, species. The salmon would leave the river at about six-inch size and do the rest of their feeding and growing in the reservoir.

It was admitted that we couldn't expect much river fishing for them. In most systems, a limited number of landlocks will run a short way upriver just after ice-out, and a scattering of fish may ascend a few miles if there's sustained high water in the summer. The major upstream migration would be a spawning run in October after the season had closed. The reservoir, which was open to the public and which the state felt was currently underutilized, would be the main fishery.

Of course, our consent wasn't necessary—state conservation personnel can enter private property at any time to check on licenses and on possible fish and game violations. However, it was tactful and considerate of the department to tell us in advance, before we stumbled on crews stocking our waters with alien fish.

I'd caught landlocks in Maine and had found them game fish that were second only to their bigger cousins, the Atlantics. They took flies readily (if in a feeding mood), fought hard, jumped high, and made delicious eating.

The landlocked salmon, *Salmo salar sebago*, looks almost exactly like its larger, sea-run relative, *Salmo salar*, except that it often has a few more black spots. The two fishes are taxonomically identical. The most detailed dissections fail to reveal any physical differences, which lead biologists to believe that landlocks split off from Atlantics quite recently.

There must be a distinct difference in genetics, however. Landlocks will not seek out salt water, but will settle for a deep lake or impoundment and do their growing up in this smaller, freshwater "ocean." Then, too, landlocks will take and digest food as they run upriver in spring or summer, while Atlantics won't. But, except for these two characteristics, their freshwater lives are similar.

Both are born in rivers and lead essentially troutlike existences until they reach six inches. This usually takes two years, but in stingy environments it can take three, even four. When this size or age is reached, the fish turn silvery, are called "smolts," and, usually in May or June, migrate downstream—Atlantics to the ocean, landlocks to their lake.

In both environments, it takes two more years of feeding and growing to attain sexual maturity. At that point, they seek out their natal river for spawning. In most Canadian rivers, Atlantics start their upriver trip as early as June, giving anglers up to four full months of river fishing. Landlocks are not nearly as accommodating. A few spawners may start nosing their way upriver in September, but most come up in a last-minute rush in October and November.

During their two-year lake-feeding period, landlocks will grow to two or three pounds, which is impressive since it took them that much time to reach two ounces in the river. The ocean is a far more lavish provider and an Atlantic salmon of the same age will weigh about ten pounds. However, both fish have the opportunity to grow much larger because, unlike the Pacific salmons, they don't necessarily die after spawning. Since they are true trouts (remember, the first names are *Salmo*), they can live on to feed, grow, and spawn several times. Both species have a life expectancy of eight years, and most are only four at first spawning. The world-record landlock weighed twenty-two and a half pounds. Atlantics have been caught weighing in at over sixty.

During the first two years of the stocking program, late-spring plantings were made with fingerlings raised from Atlantic parents of the Grand Cascapedia strain from Quebec. This gamble was taken because it was not until the third year that true landlocked stock became available. It turned out to be a poor bet. Over twenty years before, Hewitt had stocked the Neversink with fry from Scottish Atlantic salmon, and only a handful were caught or even seen in the next few years. Apparently, smolts of Atlantic parentage can't be tricked by the deep reservoir and keep on heading for salt water—either over the dam spillway or through the ten-foot-diameter water supply pipe that is armed with lethal generator turbines.

The first genetically suitable fingerlings weren't stocked until 1977. Some twenty thousand were placed in the West Branch exclusively, beginning way up in the narrow reaches seven or eight miles above the confluence. One stocker told me how they carefully tucked each tiny fish behind a protecting rock. "We planted them like kernels of corn."

This and subsequent stockings were a venturesome, even visionary, effort. Landlocks have only once been established outside their original range (in South America, of all places) and some efforts have failed even within it. Native populations were limited to northern New York, the top half of New England, and on up into New Brunswick and Quebec. Even within this limited perimeter, only some of the lake-river systems supported salmon populations.

The reason for this is that landlocks demand a highly specialized environment. First, they need a deep, cool lake with enough oxygen in the lower layers of water so they can escape the summer heat-up by cruising around at twenty- to fifty-foot depths where temperatures stay in the fifties. Nearly all qualifying lakes in the upper Northeast also contain healthy populations of smelts—another formerly anadromous species that was presumably cut off from the ocean by the same event that isolated landlocks.

Unfortunately, there are not now, nor have there ever been, lakes or rivers where landlocks are truly abundant because habitat requirements limit their numbers. Most deep, cool lakes lie at high elevations, up near the headwaters of rivers or lake-chains. At these altitudes, inlet streams are characteristically small, providing limited nursery acreage for parr and smolt to stock the lake below. Even systems that receive supplementary stockings of hatchery smolts deliver a discouraging fish-per-fishing-hour ratio. Perhaps, as is the case with muskellunge, scarcity has made landlocks even more admired and sought after.

During the first few years of this program, fingerlings were stocked in the West Branch only, but after a while in the main stem as well. Samples collected by electrical shocking revealed that fish planted into the less-fertile headwaters took three to four years to grow into six-inch smolts, whereas fish stocked in bigger water smoltified at two.

In a year or two, everyone reported hooking into small, bright fish that were obviously miniature salmon. They were most often taken from fast, almost white, water and these silvery slivers would leap several times before they could be grabbed and released. Anglers were catching yearling parr as well, but most confused them with the small trout they closely resemble.

A few years later, mature landlocks were seen and a few actually caught in the lower reaches of the river. Then, in the early 1980s, came the banner year when many salmon ascended the river in mid-June and stayed up for two or more weeks. The river had risen four feet and stayed high for several days. When it fell back to fishable height, upriver anglers started catching bright fifteen- to twenty-inch salmon as far as three or four miles up the West Branch.

We all rejoiced, convinced that this blessed event would recur after every high water now that the fish had been established. It was not to be. Occasionally, a few landlocks will nose two or three miles upriver after a summer spate, but for some inscrutable reason that major run has never been repeated.

I do catch a few larger-than-smolt-sized salmon on my water each season, but they're not a significant addition to the fishery. Some of these, in the eight- to thirteen-inch category, are fish that simply forgot to smoltify and remain troutlike in size and coloration due to a lapse in instinct. A few times each year I hook into, even catch, an obvious reservoir dweller that has moved up on high water and settled into a lie of his liking. The best of these measured just over twenty-three inches and nearly caused coronary arrest when he jumped after being hooked halfway up Cliff Pool.

These accidental fish nearly always lie in the deepest water, and since they're not addicted to overhead cover, as big browns are, they're frequently seen hovering just above the gravel. Most of the few that are caught each season are taken on minnow-imitating streamer flies when river levels are up. However, salmon will surface feed when there's a decent hatch of flies, and I've taken several up to three pounds on a size 14 dry fly and two-pound-test tippet. Needless to say, many more have broken off.

Landlocks are the most sudden of freshwater fishes and usually hit a streamer with the wallop of a barracuda. They'll surge up through five or six feet of water and zip back to the bottom so quickly you'd miss the entire show if you blinked. Such takes nearly yank the rod out of your hand, and I have seen salmon of three pounds or less snap eight-pound-test nylon when an angler had a tight grip on his line and his rod tip low.

Quickness is also the hallmark of the fight that follows. Landlocks seldom run far—I've caught only a few that got into my backing—but they're nimble and powerful broken-field runners, darting this way and that so suddenly that if you're focusing on where your line enters the water, you may catch their next jump only out of the corner of your eye.

Three or four clean, high leaps are only average performances. Some will erupt again and again like trampoline artists. It takes a prime, wild rainbow to challenge their acrobatics.

The Reverend Henry Van Dyke, America's most respected, perhaps even revered, outdoor writer back in Victorian days, positively gushed over the performance of this fish:

"Thou art not to be measured by quantity but by quality and thy
five pounds of pure vigor will outweigh a score of pounds of flesh

less vitalized by spirit. Thou feedest on the flies of the air, and thy food is transformed into an aerial passion for flight, as thou spring-est across the pool, vaulting toward the sky."

How any apostrophe as fruity as that escaped the editor's scissors I can't imagine, however it is pellucidly clear that the good reverend considered the landlock the Lord's most inspired creation since the fashioning of Eve.

After five or six years of planting young-of-the-year in running water, the state decided to shortcut this labor-intensive practice. Since the Adirondack hatchery could turn out six-inch smolts in a year, it was decided to put three thousand of these directly into the reservoir each May. Every fishlet was fin-clipped, alternating fins each year for genera-tion identification, and catches soon proved that survival rates of these direct-deposit salmon were far higher than among the more vulnerable two-month-olds placed in the demanding, fast-water environment.

The reservoir is usually ice-free by the first week in April, and landlocks have been caught as early as that. Salmon, however, like trout, rarely feed actively until the water heats up to 45 degrees, and fishing is far more productive two weeks later.

Then, too, smelt start spawning at these same temperatures and many salmon follow the huge schools inshore to the mouths of the brooks where smelt will ascend at night to lay their eggs. This is the time of great opportunity for the fly-fisher. When the salmon are within casting range in the shallows, a Grey Ghost streamer or other proven smelt imitation accounts for most catches.

Reservoir fishing holds up pretty well until surface temperatures climb up into the low sixties and hold there a few days. This usually occurs about Memorial Day, and after that the fish head out for deeper, cooler water.

This ends the fly-fishing for that spring, but a few diehards pursue landlocks all summer long. This means working the reservoir in a rowboat and trolling with lead-core line or a down-rigger. A few anglers drift-fish with a live alewife weighted down with split-shot so it will sink into fish-holding depths. Both systems seem to work, and an occasional large brown trout can sweeten the pot.

I have tried this fishing a few times, but my heart is not in it, much as I love catching salmon. Long hours under a blazing sun thrill me not, and blank days are as common as catches.

On weekends I'll often count as many as two dozen anglers along the banks live-baiting or spin casting for trout and smallmouth bass, but I can't remember ever seeing more than four boats at any one time out over the deeps where the landlocks hang out. Motors aren't permitted by the Bureau of Water Supply and horny-handed toil is not as popular as it used to be.

Reservoir stocking is considered a success by the state despite the mediocre catches. Landlocks are nowhere numerous and there are few fisheries, even up in Maine, where you're likely to do much better.

I have some misgivings about this new program, though. It seems likely that fewer of these fish will nose up into the river in spring and summer, and they may not even be attracted to the river at spawning time.

The late Dwight Webster, the foremost cold-water fishery biologist of his day, once told me that on an Adirondack fishery he supervised, landlocks stocked directly into the lake rarely located the running-water spawning area. Apparently, like Atlantics, these fish have to be imprinted in infancy by the specific and distinctive chemicals of their natal stream, otherwise it will exert little attraction.

This possibility doesn't seem to bother the state in the least. If the reservoir turned into a purely put-and-take fishery, it wouldn't make any difference to them as long as the boat and bank fishermen didn't complain. After all, how many riparian voters were there upriver? A dozen, possibly two, at most.

Still, the river keeps producing a good supply of smolts and I'm not convinced their numbers have peaked. Every fall, the retired biologist and I try to count the number of salmon that are spawning upriver. During the last few years about fifty pairs have made the trip. This means that over ten thousand eggs will be deposited, but that couldn't produce the nearly thirty thousand fry they used to stock.

Even so, this annual run makes a fascinating spectacle and nearly, but not quite, makes up for the sparse numbers of salmon upriver during the open season. They cut their redds mainly in the soft rubble bars at the tail ends of pools, the way brown trout do, and some of these fish are enormous. I have observed salmon of ten and perhaps twelve pounds spawning in early November. I've never seen such big ones in springtime.

While it is probable that most of these spawners are river-bred fish, this is hard to verify. The river is often high at this time of year and the rippled surfaces make detailed observation difficult. Identification of a fin-clip, or lack thereof, on a fish swimming in the water requires close scrutiny.

A few years back, I recalled another point Dr. Webster had brought up. Not only did spawning Atlantic salmon sniff out their parental stream, but some studies showed that they homed in on the particular portion of it where they grew up. Since pH and mineral content change as a river moves downvalley, fish can apparently be further imprinted to a relatively short, specific stretch. In other words, a salmon that grew to smolthood thirty miles up the river would run up there to spawn, whereas one that grew up only five miles above salt water would stop running and spawn there. Dr. Webster suspected that trout and landlocks probably followed the same pattern, since they are closely related and such a characteristic would be beneficial to any species by spreading its young more evenly throughout the river.

Betting that the Doctor was right, I decided to try to lure as many spawners as possible to my stretch of water. Then, when the hatched-out fry grew into smolts and finally returned as spawning adults, they would stack up in front of my house. This would offer no advantage in closed-season October, but it could be a bonanza if high water and a cold snap fooled salmon into running prematurely in September, as sometimes happens.

Making artificial spawning beds is simpler than it sounds and I'd discovered how to create them by accident. I noticed that when I'd removed all the rocks and large stones near a cribbing for use as fill, trout invariably spawned in the residual small gravel, even when current-flow and pool position made the site seem unlikely. Apparently, the proper gravel size was an overriding attraction.

Every August, now, I chuck aside all stones larger than fist size in patches where the current quickens at the tail ends of pools. If a scouring flood doesn't undo my handiwork, both salmon and brown trout find these prepared sites irresistible. In good years I have attracted as many as seventeen pairs of spawning salmon, plus a lot of browns, to my relatively short stretch of water.

The one September when we've had both unseasonably cool weather plus a good flush of water, the latter turned out to be too much of a good thing. A five-foot rise in river level, which ranks as a junior flood, scoured my prepared beds down to the large, forbidding rocks underneath.

My artificial beds will stay in mint condition through a three-foot rise, but that may not be enough flow to draw salmon up prematurely. We'll see one day. In theory my scheme should work, but it will probably do so only under a rare combination of circumstances.

Still, I can prepare six-foot by six-foot beds with about an hour's rock tossing, and two years out of three they remain so inviting that fish programmed to spawn higher up are seduced into stopping. The resulting samlets must achieve better growth and survival rates in these slower and more fertile waters. Even if I've overestimated this benefit to the fishery, just witnessing these big fish working in the shallows or resting up in the adjacent pools makes the few hours spent one of my shrewdest investments of the year.

17

Beside the Still Waters

When I was looking over the downstream property before buying it, I was so intrigued by the section of river running through it that I barely noticed its two other amenities. One of these is a four-foot-wide brook that enters the river a hundred feet upstream of my house site. Even during the direst droughts this stream continues to flow, and each of its deeper, pocketlike pools, scattered among huge boulders, contains two or three brook trout up to ten inches long. While this isn't a major fishery, it taught my boys, as youngsters, the basics of trout fishing when they worm-fished their way up it.

Just beyond the brook lies an even more valuable asset—a half-acre, spring-fed pond. Long and narrow with a right-angle bend in its middle, this is obviously either a section of old riverbed or a deep scour from a forgotten, hundred-year flood. Nowhere in its four-hundred-foot length is it more than thirty feet wide, and except for a living-room-sized pocket where it bends and holds over five feet of water, it averages only two feet deep.

It is generously supplied with spring water fed from the steep hillside behind it, some merely seeping in but, in several places, boiling up strongly from vents in the pond bottom. This gives it a surprisingly stable temperature, cool in the heat of summer and far warmer than the nearby river in winter. Since the upwellings discharge water at a constant 44 degrees in all seasons, the pond freezes over only in the bitterest weather and even then with only a thin sheet of ice.

Several beavers occupy this pond every year and have further raised the water level with a fifteen-foot-long dam across its outlet to the river. Since there are so few still waters in the Valley, the pond also attracts a large number of muskrats, herons, and ducks. Mallards and wood ducks pile in during spring and fall migrations and supply me with choice fly-tying materials plus a few gourmet feasts each autumn.

Needless to say, brook trout love these cool, still waters, too. Some are born and raised here, while many river dwellers manage to slither through or over the dam in autumn to spawn in the spring flows. On opening day, April 1, I can invariably catch a few brookies there in celebration of the great event weeks before the river begins to produce.

Every fall I count dozens of brook trout digging redds up both arms and this must be ideal spawning territory because each spring there are literally thousands of troutlets darting around in the shallows. Due to the relatively warm water in winter, egg development is speeded up, and I have found fry in the pond as early as Washington's Birthday—nearly two months before I see the first hatchlings in the river margins.

There's only one minor fault with this pond: It's not flood-free. When river levels rise five feet, which they usually do at least once each year, the pond mixes with the floodwaters and there is a resulting exchange of fish. A lot of the brookies retreat up the arm farthest from the river to avoid the roily currents, and thereby remain residents. Sometimes salmon parr and brown trout from the river seek the same sanctuary and are trapped by the receding waters. Once a two-pound brown had to spend the entire summer in this lockup, and he was so disgruntled he wouldn't touch any fly I offered him.

Twice I have stocked this pond with Tamiscamies-strain brook trout. The first time, I put in three- to four-inch young-of-the-year fish in early October. We had a major flood before the season opened the following spring, which may have flushed most of them out into the harsher world of the river. I didn't recapture a single one out of the pond that summer, although I'll admit I didn't fish it very often. I didn't catch any of them out of the adjacent river, either, and I examined every brookie I caught for a telltale, clipped adipose fin.

Two years later I tried again with a spring stocking of yearlings seven to nine inches long, and again with the adipose fin removed for identification. These fish grew a couple of inches during the summer and made up about 25 percent of my pond catch until the season closed at the end of September. As with my previous transplants, I caught no marked trout from either pond or river the following year.

Where all these Tamiscamies migrated to is still a mystery. While biologists told me to expect an annual mortality rate of 50 percent for the yearlings and perhaps 75 to 80 percent for young-of-the-year fish, that still left a lot of trout unaccounted for. Perhaps the AWOLs were swept to other sections downriver, or even into the reservoir itself. Survival rates in the more testing river environment would necessarily be lower than those quoted for ponds. Still, I think the odds are that a few of these potentially outsized fish, or ones from earlier stockings, have survived and spawned.

I fished the pond only occasionally during my first few years downriver—usually only when the river was too high—and considered it mainly a duck-hunting bonus. Having seen those "Attract Wild Ducks" ads in outdoor magazines, I promptly sent for several kinds of seeds and tubers for transplanting. Wild rice, which would also have made ideal stuffing for ducks, turned out to be a total failure. Watercress, I found, could be established near strong, spring inflows, but most years muskrats pulled it out before it got well-rooted enough to spread. The one permanent success has been sago pondweed. Each season, this clogs one of the upper arms of the pond with its dark green filaments and small, white, emergent flowers. Ducks flock to this section every fall, and on some gunning dawn patrols I have seen as many as two dozen wood ducks feeding in this patch. One time they flushed in flights of four at about one-second intervals, making an accurate count easy. I was so startled by the splash of jumping ducks and the whirr of wings that I never shouldered my gun. I was a bit better prepared for the pairs that came back for seconds that evening.

One year I fed lights to the pond fish religiously, starting in early April, and though returns were satisfying, they weren't astonishing. By September I was catching trout a full foot long—the top size in previous years had been ten inches—and fish of all sizes were much plumper than usual.

Feeding lights in the pond as well as in the river was a chore with a low priority because the pond was only a minor fishery, and in the ensuing years it dropped off to a hit-or-miss activity. Still, it was a program of some value since many pond fish would wind up in the river after a flood, and the bigger and fatter they started out the better.

The ideal solution, I felt, would be a self-feeding mechanism for the pond. The sago pondweed, though firmly established and spreading slowly, wasn't much help in this area. It was great duck fodder, but it didn't harbor much insect life. Tall and stringy with sparse, filamentous leaves, it offered minimum algae pasturage and even less concealment for shrimps, scuds, and insects.

I'd learned that I couldn't transplant weeds into the river, but I thought that perhaps the pond, with its lack of currents and with a rich muck bottom—the end product of decades of decaying leaf mold—might be more hospitable. There were only two problems: Which type of weed would harbor the most animal life, and where could I obtain it?

The few times I'd fished the slow compensation flow below the reservoir-dam, I'd noticed the riverbed was paved with several types of waterweed. The metered and flood-free flow apparently allowed many types of vegetation to root, spread, and prosper. Though the pH of the water was still slightly acidic, the streambed masqueraded as a chalk stream. Most important of all, this lush growth produced huge hatches of small to tiny mayflies nearly all day long in spring, and almost every evening in summer.

Many of the weed types in this lower river were obviously unsuitable—long and stringy, offering no sanctuary and sure to catch your leader when they grew up to the surface, vertically, in still water. Samples plucked from the stream bottom and examined proved such weeds were virtually barren of insect life.

Some dark, blue-green mosses, two in particular, looked promising, though. Both grew in large patches, hugged the stream bottom, and attained a maximum length of only six inches. One that looked slightly greenish had coarse, pulpy fronds, while the other, looking almost black on the riverbed, had extremely dense clumps of hairlike leaves.

I pulled up equal-sized clumps of both types and laid them out side by side on a driftwood board for closer scrutiny. As the water drained away I noticed signs of life in both samples, and about a minute later, after most of the clinging water had puddled onto the board below, activity became almost frenetic. In fact, the darker of the two mosses, the one with the finer foliage, became so active I thought it was going to crawl off the board. Subsequent tests confirmed that this moss was twice as densely populated as the one with the succulent foliage.

An inventory of this underwater zoo turned up some surprises. For instance, by far the most numerous animals were scuds of all sizes up to three quarters of an inch, and which look much like those pill bugs you find in rotting wood. These make superb trout food and I'd had no idea they were present in such great numbers because, unlike aquatic insects, they don't hatch out and advertise themselves by flying around. There were also a fair number of freshwater shrimps that I hadn't expected.

Then too, there was the anticipated goodly supply of small mayfly nymphs plus quite a few caddises. About the only superior trout food I didn't find were small, freshwater snails. Apparently there just weren't enough carbonates in the water to permit shell-building.

The next weekend I came back and filled two buckets with clumps of the preferred moss. Its roots were weak, shallow, and came away with barely enough sand in their tangles to ballast them, roots down, in the new environment. Such a tenuous root structure couldn't begin to take hold out in the river currents.

Back at the pond, I tossed in the hunks of weed, scattering them at two-yard intervals, and watched them settle to the muck bottom. It didn't look like much of a planting so I went back to the river, filled the buckets again, and threw that batch in, too. Still a thin seeding, but I convinced myself that if the weed found the environment congenial it would spread readily enough, and if the pond wasn't to its liking an entire truckload would wither away.

By the following season, the clumps had multiplied in size, and by the third year they formed a wall-to-wall carpet. Pulled-up samples revealed dense populations of scuds and shrimps. There were only a few caddises, however, and I couldn't find any mayfly nymphs at all. Come to think of it, I hadn't seen any mayflies hatching out on the pond surface, either. Those insect species obviously need the constant bathing of a current and were unsuited to still-water life. Nevertheless, I had to consider that, overall, my pond food-production program was a roaring success.

This extra food supply certainly improved trout fishing in the pond, but in a way that was somewhat disappointing. While the numbers of trout the pond supports has appreciated considerably, their size has remained surprisingly constant. A ten-incher is still a big one and there are no eleven-inchers. It appears that brook trout are not greedy feeders that compete aggressively. Extra calories simply mean that more young-of-the-year survive, not that the dominant fish grow bigger. Brookies seem to regulate their lives on the "lifeboat" principle.

I probably should have expected this size limitation in my wild brook trout population. Years before, I had been a member of the second group ever to fish a small lake in Canada that had just been opened up by a new logging road. After a horrendous trip up what shouldn't have been called a road at all, we arrived at the lake and pushed off on the raft left by the loggers ahead of us.

On this nearly virgin water we hooked trout on every cast, and when we added two dropper flies we often landed triples. In a few hours we each caught several hundred brookies. We killed only a few that were hooked so deeply they couldn't possibly have survived. However, out of that sample of perhaps a thousand fish, not a one measured over a foot. Except where predators like pike thin their ranks, brook trout convert the available food supply into the most fish rather than the largest. Only by pouring on the lights and force-feeding my fish had I been able to push my trout over the ten-inch barrier.

This increase in pond food and population had a ripple effect on my entire fishery. The exchange of fish due to flooding greatly increased the number of brook trout in the nearby section of the river as well. Fishing guests from other sections of the main-stem river are amazed at the number of brook trout in my water.

During major floods, which occur every few years, currents are strong enough to rip out sections of the moss bed, and I then try to speed up the healing process by reseeding bare patches with clumps from surviving beds. I don't know where this flotsam weed ends up. Stranded in some woods downriver, I'd guess, or perhaps washed into the reservoir. I certainly don't expect to find anything that weakly rooted miraculously transplanted and thriving in the riverbed downstream.

But what about all those scuds and shrimp that are also washed into the river? These animals produce several large generations of young each season, and it wouldn't take more than a small cadre of survivors to build up large populations in the river if conditions were receptive.

I had been lead to believe that a pond rich in animal life would trickle food into its adjoining river through its outlet stream. Carter Platts, in his instructive book *Trout Streams and Salmon Rivers*, recommended the damming back of trickles into small still waters and stocking them with weeds, shrimps, and insect larvae as a natural way to add food to a trout stream.

Well, that may have worked on the English moorland streams where Platts made his river improvements, but it doesn't work on the Neversink. I have never found any shrimps or scuds in the pond's short outlet stream, nor have I ever found any in the bellies of river-dwelling trout.

Under normal water conditions, scuds and shrimp seem content in their weed beds and show no urge to climb over the beaver dam and explore the rocky river below. When their home beds are uprooted and sluiced into the river, water levels are so high that all self-respecting trout are tucked under rock slabs, more concerned with surviving than with eating, and this extra food simply goes to waste. All the evidence indicates that while the improved pond stocks the river with trout, it contributes little or nothing to it in the way of trout food.

18

Wind and Weather

The one great blessing of my dual residency—a home in New York City and another on the Neversink—is that I experience two distinct and separate springtimes. It almost, but not quite, compensates me for the agonies of Friday and Sunday night traffic this coming and going imposes.

I don't ask for two summers. I get five months or more of warm to hot weather in New York anyway. Only a fanatic skier would want two icy winters. And I don't expect two falls because we don't have even one in the city. It simply gets colder and a few grubby leaves appear underfoot and you can't call that a fall.

But two springs! In late March I start seeing snowdrops, hyacinths, and daffodils in sunny front-yard gardens in Greenwich Village. Then, by the first week in April, the flowering Callery pear trees that line nearby Greenwich Street turn into chalk-white clouds, and scattered crab apples show pink-and-white blossoms a few days later.

During this same period, the high Catskills are still stark and barren. It's not until late April that the first green plants, false hellebores, poke up in the floodplain, and the grasses in lawns or fields rarely green up until nearly the first of May. Fruit trees don't flower up here until mid-May, and last season the blossoms hadn't completely opened by May 20. Hardwoods are rarely in full canopy until Memorial Day. Thus, my season of hope and promise extends over two delicious months.

While the entire Catskill region averages several degrees cooler than New York City because it is both higher and farther from the warming influence of the ocean, the upper Neversink Valley is cold even by Catskill standards. Altitude plays some part in this: The reservoir stands at 1,440 feet, and the pass into the next valley at Winnisook is over 2,800 feet. Then too, the Neversink Valley is more shaded than others nearby. There are relatively few open fields for the sun to beat down on, and the extensive overstory of mature hardwoods and conifers exerts a cooling influence, at least in summer.

But I feel there's something more involved here. I'm convinced a third factor is at work: a minimistral. Cold air from Slide Mountain, the high peak at the head of both of our valleys, slides south down the Neversink the way cold air from the Alps funnels down the Rhône Valley to the Mediterranean.

I pointed out earlier that it is this extra measure of coolness that perpetuates the Neversink as a major brook trout fishery, but it does more than that. It adds many days to the viable fishing season. Warmer, neighboring rivers may, indeed, provide hatching flies and fly-fishing in early April, while it's rare to see any kind of hatch on the Neversink before May Day. However, these lost days are refunded in extra measure when things heat up. During many weeks in July and August nearby rivers can be too hot for anything except, possibly, night fishing. On the other hand, I have never, even during heat waves, seen temperatures on the Neversink rise high enough to put the damper on either morning or evening fishing.

I well remember one Memorial Day weekend when I woke up to

find four inches of snow on the ground. Ten inches had accumulated on the surrounding hills and in the uppermost reaches of the Valley, and the river ran red with runoff for two days while this blanket melted.

Just last year, my newly transplanted tomato plants were blackened by a killing frost the night of June 7. A few years back, every tomato in the Valley that hadn't been prudently covered overnight was killed by frost in mid-August. July is the only month of the year during which below-freezing temperatures haven't been recorded.

The weather bureau reports that the mean annual temperature of New York City is a fraction above 53 degrees. I have seen no such figure for our valley, but it can't be over 40 degrees and perhaps it's a shade lower.

All this is bad news for tomatoes, string beans, squash, and year-round residents, but it's a boon to summer soldiers retreating from the heat of city streets. Nighttime temperatures predictably drop into the fifties even in the middle of July, and on clear nights the mid-forties are not unusual. I can recall only two freak, muggy nights in all these years when I didn't welcome at least one light wool blanket on my bed.

Winter conditions, as you might imagine, can be accurately described as cruel. Nighttime readings of twenty below zero or less are common during cold snaps. One Thanksgiving we were hit with two feet of snow which kept deer hunters housebound for three frustrating days. You can expect to trudge through corn snow lying under the evergreens if you're impatient enough to try the river on the trout season's opener, which appropriately coincides with April Fool's Day.

Chalky green runoff known as snow water characteristically colors the river until late in April, and you can't expect water temperatures to climb out of the thirties until all the snow has melted off the surrounding mountains. Even the few live-bait fishers—usually poachers—come home empty-handed during the early season.

Although the entire Valley has a well-earned reputation as a cold spot—a small cluster of buildings up the West Branch appears on road maps as "Frost Valley"—the upper reaches are even cooler than the lower elevations. This temperature regression is seldom noticed by city weekenders, but plants unerringly respond to the subtle change. As you travel up the Valley, you can make out changes in the vegetation—some species dropping out while new ones begin to take over.

19

Green Things

During my first year on the Neversink, the Queen of the West Branch had told me that there was no poison ivy in the upper Valley and I'm now convinced this is the case. Neither I nor anyone I know has ever found any of those shiny green leaves above the reservoir, although there are plenty of them not far below it. Apparently it's just too cold up there for that unpleasant plant to establish itself or survive.

Unfortunately, this is nearly true of the wild grapes that ruffed grouse can't resist in October. There are three clumps on my property at the 1,550-foot contour mark, but I have never found another vine upriver of that. My plants have Tarzan-sized stalks running up tree trunks to the canopies above and look to be extremely old. Despite their great size, however, they appear to have a tenuous hold on life. They do produce fair crops of fruit each season, but they're unable to spread or multiply. Search as I will, I have yet to find either a volunteer seedling or young shoot.

There is another invisible boundary farther upriver at about 1,700 feet. Below this elevation butternut and red oak trees are fairly common, but they dwindle rapidly above it. The only nut-bearing trees in the higher valley are the beeches that threaten to take over large sections of hillside. I can't decide whether this is a benefit or a bane. Beeches are, perhaps, the least valuable of the local hardwoods. On the other hand, beechnuts are a staple late-fall and winter food for deer, wild turkey, grouse, and squirrels.

In any event, areas that have been heavily logged tend to grow back as pure beech forests. Deer browse off the tender shoots of other hardwood seedlings, but find beech saplings bitter or distasteful. I have never conducted a taste test on new-growth twigs so I'll have to accept the deer's verdict.

As if in compensation, balsam firs make their appearance at this level and gradually increase in abundance as you continue upvalley. Near the top of Slide Mountain—not technically in the Valley, but certainly within the Neversink drainage basin—you begin to find stands of that far-northern tree, the red spruce.

Most trees exhibit a wider tolerance of temperature and elevation variations. White pines, hemlocks, beeches, maples, and yellow birches thrive in the Valley from top to bottom.

Several shorter, shrubby plants always beat the major hardwoods in leafing out. Red elder and shinhobble are out early and so are the brushy willows that line the banks of wide, sunny stretches of the river.

I am no botanist or even wildflower collector, but certain plants command my attention because they act as milestones that mark the progress of the season far more accurately than does the calendar with those too-good-to-be-true naked ladies the local garage hands out.

For instance, when the bush willows in front of my house take on a distinct, greenish tinge, I know I finally have a fighting chance to take a trout on either a weighted, artificial nymph or a streamer fly. This usually occurs about May Day, but the magic moment can fall up to a week either side of that date. The hours of direct sunshine and mean temperature so far that season are relayed with uncanny accuracy to the angler by vegetation.

Another signal is sent to me by the adder's-tongue, or trout lily, and by the painted and wake-robin trilliums. When I see their flowers I know the first decent hatch of mayflies, the sooty Quill Gordons, will be on the water in early afternoon, and that dry-fly fishing has at last begun.

Similarly, when the shadbush, or serviceberry, blossoms, I expect flights of the black-brown caddis appropriately known as the shad fly. About five days later, as the apple blossoms start bursting, I know I'll see the mayfly called the Hendrickson riding down the pools, and when these petals start to drop, I can count on the appearance of the big, yellowish mayflies called Grey Foxes, which promise the biggest, most productive mayfly hatches of the season. The last major insect event of spring—the swarming of dark blue caddises—will start when the laggard oaks are finally in full leaf.

Summer wildflowers are too profuse to catalogue and none mark events of importance to me. My wife can identify most of them and presses blossoms and leaves of the less common ones between the pages of heavy books. Surplus plants are arranged into bouquets that brighten up the house.

I don't raise any domestic flowers in my garden. Nature provides more than we can use at this time of year. Rototilling, weeding, and watering are such a chore that I've adopted a gardening philosophy of "If you can't eat it, to hell with it."

A few summer blooms are so spectacular that even I have to take notice of them. Bee balm is one. So is the jewelweed that grows in mucky patches on the margins of my pond. Then there's the foxglove, an escape from a formal garden upriver, I'm told, that lines the river in front of my house. Their large, multicolored and conical flower clusters confirm that full summer is here.

Even more showy are the blossoming wild rhododendrons expected by the first week in July. In protected places—notably precipitous banks the deer won't climb to browse back the plants in winter—these white-and-pink flowers create the floral event of the year. Nowhere, not even in the tropics, have I witnessed a more ostentatious display.

Blossoms also announce less welcome days. The first bad-news flower of the season is the purple loosestrife that ushers in August—the month that, for some reason, brings the poorest fishing of the season. There's little loosestrife in our valley and that's a blessing because this European transplant offers no food value to any bird or animal, yet aggressively shoulders out damp-loving species that do. During my comings and goings, though, I see abandoned fields in Orange County blanketed with these electric-purple flowers, and it's saddening to realize that a spectacle this lavish promises hard times for wildlife.

When goldenrod fills untended meadows—not just its first yellow flecks, but when fields are fully gilded with it—I expect a killing frost and, a couple of weeks later, the closing of trout season. Come to think of it, I'd held a grudge against goldenrod long before I entered the Valley. By my early teens, I'd learned that this yellow carpet signaled good-bye to the tight-skinned, honey-haired girls of summer and a return to books and the daily bruisings of football.

Goldenrod flowers also coincide with the first coloring in the hills. Yellow birches and odd branches of maple catch fire at this time. Ashes and beeches soon follow suit and the oaks, typically, are the last to turn.

Colors peak at the end of September, drawing carloads of "leaf peepers" through the Valley. This show, especially in bright sunshine, tops even the fruit-tree blossomings of spring, but that's a bitter compensation. I can't rejoice at the death of yet another year.

The first mid-October rain pelts most leaves to the ground, opening up the woods for grouse hunters. By the time November comes in, the woods will be winter-bare. Only beech saplings and oaks now show any foliage and this they will retain all through the winter.

Evergreens shed during this season, though less spectacularly. Starting on Labor Day, hemlocks drop their small needles into the river, but despite the insect shapes of the needles, the trout aren't fooled into taking them for slim beetles. White pines shed about a month later, dropping a third of their foliage each year and creating a golden mulch underfoot.

I can't sign off on Valley vegetation without a word of praise for an unspectacular and unsung plant: the sedge grass that lines sections of riverbank. This is easy to distinguish from the wild grasses because its stems are triangular in cross section and grow in ottoman-sized hummocks. These provide elegant seating for anglers watching the water for rises, or changing flies, and play a major role in stabilizing banks. Their root systems are nearly as well-entrenched as the willow's and they'll grow in spots too shady for that bush to gain a foothold.

Their nearly black seeds form clusters much like ears of wheat and start shedding about Memorial Day. When I see windrows of their grain stranded along the river margins, I tread them into the wet sand and gravel to help them germinate. Once mature plants are established, only the lethal plow of a large tree's rootball can tear them out.

20

The Birds and the Beasts

Not only is the Valley without a trace of poison ivy, it is free of poisonous snakes as well. Nobody has ever identified either a rattlesnake or a copperhead up there, although rattlers are fairly common about twenty miles below the reservoir near Bridgeville. Nearly every year someone claims to have seen a "copperhead" around Claryville, but it always turns out to be a pine or milk snake of similar color pattern, but without the triangular head of a pit viper. Even these false-alarm reptiles are uncommon, although we do have a fair supply of garter snakes.

Nobody gives Saint Patrick credit for this poison-free miracle—it's just considered one of the few compensations for living in an icebox. Turtles are rare also, but this may be due more to the lack of standing water than to temperature. Perhaps that also explains why there aren't many frogs either.

In fact, Valley residents rarely worry about being bitten or poisoned by anything. There are surprisingly few mosquitoes, although I'll admit you may have to swat one or two in the evening if there's been a prolonged, summer rainy spell. We do get two or three weeks of blood-letting black flies in late May and early June, but their numbers are modest compared with the *Luftwaffes* that patrol the Maine woods. No-see-ums, or biting midges, can be annoying at dawn and dusk—especially down by the river—but their bites don't swell up and itch so their harrassment is only temporary.

Most of our larger beasts are benign, too, at least as far as their intentions toward human beings are concerned. A few black bears prowl the Valley each summer, and while they can scare the culottes off lady berry-pickers, the few I've encountered raced off in mortal terror of little old me.

Deer are abundant to the point of being pests, and young fruit trees and vegetable gardens need at least five feet of wire fencing for protection. Of course, hunters try to convert these beasts into venison every fall, but there are so many large, tightly-posted estates in the Valley that hunting doesn't cull the deer population as much as a winter with deep snowfall will.

Around houses, gardens, and orchards, deer can appear so domesticated, even brazen, that Bambi-ists have been heard to exclaim, "How could anyone ever shoot one of those lovely, tame creatures?" My reply to that is, "It ain't easy." These animals have come to accept my presence near the house, but if I try to approach the same deer a short distance away in the woods, ninety-nine times out of a hundred he'll slink or bolt away before I'm within gunshot range.

About twenty years ago, coyotes, or coydogs, moved into the Valley from the north. They look much like German shepherd dogs and usually hunt in packs. They're quite shy—you rarely see them—but you often hear a chorus of howling nearby just at dark. This is slightly unnerving, but the game warden promises that it's deer, not me, they're after. As I stumble back to the house after fishing until dark some nights, I keep telling myself the pack heard the warden as clearly as I did.

Some claim these animals are neither coyotes nor coydogs. I read an article a few years ago that maintained these are actually coywolves. Decades ago, when the over-hunted coyotes of the West looped back to less-harrassed eastern areas, they migrated through northern Minnesota and southern Ontario and bred with resident gray wolves rather than domestic dogs. The evidence cited was that a dog—coyote offspring is whelped in February and can't survive winter weather north of Virginia. A coyote—wolf liaison, however, produces litters in April—a viable month even in the chilly Neversink Valley. I take no great comfort in learning that our local packs may be half-wolf rather than half-Pekingese.

Every few years, someone claims to have sighted a mountain lion in the Valley, and several of these eyewitnesses have been both knowledgeable and reliable. Descriptions of tawny animals about four feet long with flat, catlike faces and long ropey tails from experienced outdoorsmen who are also respected executives or professionals can't be dismissed lightly. State biologists admit there may be a few panthers in the Adirondacks, but doubt there are any as far south as the Catskills. That's fine with me. I'm not sure I need hundred-pound-plus carnivores lurking in the bushes nearby while I'm concentrating on a rising trout.

We certainly have bobcats, though. I'll admit I've never encountered one face-to-face in our valley, but I find sets of their distinctive tracks each year. Since these predators wander over a wide area, they may be merely passing through. They are reported to have a preference for cottontail and snowshoe rabbits, and since we have only small populations of these species, we may not host many resident wildcats, either.

Foxes we have in abundance—mostly handsome reds, but a few grays, as well. Several times, while on a deer stand, I have watched them forage within thirty feet of me, sniffing, then pawing, under boulders, obviously searching for mice and voles. They are colorful, frisky animals, but they're much smaller than I'd thought. I doubt that one would weigh more than ten pounds wringing wet.

As I mentioned earlier, the Valley is loaded with raccoons, and since nobody around here hunts or traps them, they are a persistent nuisance. They love to tip over unsecured garbage cans and scatter the contents. Sweet corn attracts them like a magnet. They'll wait until the ears are just ripe enough for eating, then break down the stalks and strip the ears. They'll eat their fill, vomit up their stomach contents, then fill up again like ancient Romans at a banquet. I have given up trying to grow my own corn on the cob.

Skunks are uncommon—I've seen less than half a dozen in all these years and only a few road kills. I presume they find it hard to eke out a living with so many raccoons around scavenging for the same type of food.

I had always considered possums denizens of the Deep South and had never seen one in the Northeast until well after World War II. In the last few decades they have invaded the North and are now common even in our cold valley. I have yet to see one during daylight—they're essentially nocturnal—but the number of road kills suggest they're now nearly as numerous as coons.

Porcupines are surprisingly scarce and I can't understand why. There are enough trees around to support an army of them. I can't say I'd look forward to an increase in these comatose, lumbering beasts, though. They once made a shambles of the doorframe and front stoop of my parents' summer cottage in New Hampshire, and they're especially bad news for dog-owners.

I have a smoldering hatred for the woodchucks that burrow in the corners of every vacant field. They never touch my garden in June, when most seedlings, except early lettuce, are small. But in July, when I'm convinced my defenses are chuck-proof, they burrow under my buried fencing while I'm away in the city and, in three or four days of uninterrupted foraging, lay waste to my produce.

I have had years to study their habits and preferences. Their first choice is always broccoli. Next they focus on brussels sprouts and string beans, using lettuce as a side dish. They nibble down the carrot tops only when they've polished off their other favorites. Fortunately, they rarely bother squash, cucumbers, tomatoes, onions, asparagus, or beets.

This year I installed my Maginot Line. I scrounged sheets of discarded tin roofing, sank them two feet deep, and laced five-foot-high chicken wire to the barely protruding top rims. *Ils ne passeront pas!*

Beavers are only a minor annoyance in comparison. Weekend guests who don't fish often spend evenings watching the beavers work on their dam. They're accustomed to people and keep on fetching and placing twigs and branches and slapping on mud patches as long as you stay about fifty feet away. Young children especially enjoy this show, and their parents can't help pointing out the moral lessons to be learned from the beaver's compulsive industry.

What they don't know is that this construction material comes from trees that once shaded my trout pond. Rather than commuting to the river for willows, they take my basswood, white ash, and yellow birch. Then, seemingly out of malice, they girdle hemlocks without felling them, leaving them to die upright. I guess I should be grateful that they don't like white pines, sycamores, oaks, or maples.

Muskrats are freeloaders, moving in to build their tunnel-dens in the banks of the still waters backed up by workaholic beavers. They're attractive animals that keep on lugging mouthfuls of vegetation back to their young in the burrows even while I'm in plain view. My only complaint with them is that they're overly fond of watercress, and if I want to be sure of a regular supply of garnish I have to place a screen cage over at least one sizable clump.

The mink and otters that patrol the river have already been described, but I should touch on our squirrels. We have average numbers of three species: gray, red, and flying. The first two are fun to watch and mind their own business out of doors, but flying squirrels make nests each year in the ceiling above my bedroom. The builder of my house has examined the exterior in that area and can't find any holes, gaps, or slits for them to get through. They always manage to, however, and every dawn and dusk I'm treated to a quarter-hour track meet directly overhead.

Of course we have a host of small, brown, furry beasts: shrews, moles, mice, and voles, none of which I have ever been interested enough in to sort out, although the mice have caught my attention. Every fall, when I turn on the furnace, they invade my house in droves. These small creatures are said to be incredibly stupid, but they certainly know enough to come in out of the cold. I set several traps for them every night I'm there, and I feel I'm a failure when I don't score doubles or triples. To confound those who accuse me of being an effete purist, I'll confess I don't use artificials on them. A dab of peanut butter will outcatch a Royal Coachman ten to one.

All the above adds up to a sketchy, slipshod bestiary, but I'm not qualified to compile a definitive natural history of the Valley. If you're intrigued by matters like the social bonding in beaver families, or the exact age at which deer reach puberty, there are dozens of authoritative volumes that will give you those vital statistics.

I'm afraid my listing of Valley birds will be equally cavalier and subjective for the same reason. I have a strong prejudice in favor of game birds and raptors and observe them carefully, while I'm likely to ignore most dickey birds.

Several pairs of woodcock nest in the wooded flats near my house each season. They arrive in mid-March when snow is often on the ground, but I don't know how they can probe out worms at that time of year. I once stumbled onto one of their nests—a small depression in a clump of coarse grass containing four tan eggs with bold, chocolate streakings. I was amazed that such a small bird could lay eggs as big as a pullet's.

While woodcock tolerate our March weather, they dislike late fall. I rarely see one after November 1. A few flight birds pass through in October, but most northern and Canadian birds choose the less-arduous routes down the Hudson and Delaware valleys. These are the best of all birds for pointing-dog training. They'll hold tight within three or four feet of a dog's nose and almost never flush wild.

Our ruffed grouse have just the opposite habits and are as wild as March Hares. My late and lamented Brittany bitch was the most soft-footed dog I've ever shot over—she'd creep in like a cat when she smelled game upwind—yet even on wet days most grouse flushed twenty to thirty yards ahead of her. The majority of these birds, certainly all of the young-of-the-year, had never been shot at before, and for many it was their first encounter with a human being, so I have to conclude that this flighty trait is genetic. Close-sitting birds have been culled. The grouse I run across in Canada, on the other hand, let me get within ten feet or so of them and would hold even tighter in front of a dog.

When I first came into the Valley, flushing two dozen or more grouse in a short hunting day was the norm. Today, I consider myself fortunate if I put up four or five. My favorite covers have probably matured imperceptibly over the years and are by now too grown up to support many birds. This is a deep loss because the white-meated ruffed grouse is the finest table bird in the world.

Nearly twenty years ago the state obtained some wild turkeys from Pennsylvania and stocked them into the Catskills. These huge birds—some toms weigh over twenty pounds—have thrived on our wild nuts and insects. Now we see tracks up and down the Valley and I think the population is still increasing. Gobblers are extremely shy and usually stay out of sight and away from houses. I'll go weeks without sighting even one, and then the next weekend I'll spot two or three flocks of a dozen or more birds.

While I'm sure wild turkey is a marvelous dish, I have hunted them only twice. I'd heard it's a game that takes a lot of skill and calling practice, and the experts who have taken me out convinced me of this. However, answering the alarm clock before four in the morning and stumbling through the woods a half hour before first light doesn't intrigue me. I doubt that I have the makings of a turkey hunter.

Even the most chauvinistic Valley-booster couldn't claim it offers much to the wildfowler. In the first place, few ducks and geese fly over it because the north end of the Valley is guarded by a high pass and there's too much nearby competition. There's an easy, flat route down the Hudson to the east, and the broad Delaware Valley to the west. Then too, there's little inducement for the ducks to stop even when they pass through. There are only a handful of man-made or beaver ponds and I can't think of any marshes or swamps.

In spring, a few more ducks blunder up the Valley from its low end, but nearly all of them soon realize they've taken a wrong turn and continue northward. I have put up wood-duck boxes around my pond, but have yet to lure a pair of occupants. I rarely hear reports of mallards or woodies nesting in the Valley. But for some inscrutable reason, the murderous mergansers find our nesting conditions ideal, and hardly a day goes by in summer when I don't see at least one red-headed hen sailing downriver with a squadron of ducklings in formation behind her.

Despite this dismal picture, I do manage to kill a few ducks each fall, even though this is far from classic waterfowl shooting. In the mornings, I stalk up to the edge of my pond hoping for a jump shot at early feeders or overnighters. Evenings, I crouch in an impromptu blind, waiting for birds to return for a snack of my sago.

The only reason why I get any shooting at all is that a certain number of over-flyers stop off for a night's rest on the flat, safe waters of the reservoir. Those that aren't in a hurry to reach the Sunbelt forage locally for a day or two, and my pond is the first likely still water they see as they take the logical, upriver route. Mallards and wood ducks are most common although I do see a few teal. Two or three pairs of black ducks usually winter on the lower, unfrozen sections of the river, but these don't arrive until December.

Canada geese have much the same habits as the puddle ducks, except that most gaggles overnighting on the reservoir resume their migration the next morning. I have encountered only a few small flights making low-level explorations upriver, and usually my gun is back at the house when I make these sightings.

Ospreys and eagles I have touched on before. The eagles stay with us all winter, but the ospreys are spring and fall migrants. Seeing these huge birds at close range always raises my pulse rate and gives me the false illusion that I am, indeed, in a pristine wilderness.

Other smaller raptors are only slightly less stirring. Red-tailed and broad-winged hawks are common sights, and so are the perky kestrels that patrol the larger meadows and fields. A particular favorite of mine is that large accipiter, the goshawk. Every season I see several, and for three years in a row a pair nested on the hillside behind my house. They used my driveway, which is arched over with branches, as a tunnel route to their hunting grounds across the river. When sitting on my terrace sipping morning coffee, a blue bullet whooshing by a few feet over my head makes me wonder what would happen if I stood up suddenly at the wrong moment. I'll bet a two-pound bird racing at fifty to sixty miles per hour could snap a man's neck.

For the past few years we have had at least one pair of ravens nesting at the head of the reservoir. Their size, bell-like calls, and wedge-shaped tails rule out any chance of confusing them with crows. I have never before seen these large black birds south of Bangor, Maine. Welcome to the North woods.

We host three types of swallows: tree, bank, and barn, the latter being far the most abundant. They have an unerring knack for sensing when the first aquatic insects will hatch out. The arrival of swallows, as surely as the flowering of trilliums, tells me that trout will now take a floating fly.

Several other types of birds make their livings off our aquatic insects. As you'd expect, phoebes and kingbirds, which are classified as flycatchers, do so, but red-winged blackbirds hector flies rising off the water, too. Cedar waxwings are ardent mayfly- and caddis-catchers as well, which surprises me. Their thick bills had led me to presume they were primarily seedeaters.

Warblers devour great quantities of our river flies, mostly hunting and pecking for them in the foliage. Blackburnian, bay-breasted, and redstarts are most common around the house. The yellow warbler jumps the gun on them by hanging out in shoreline willows, fielding the emerging insects alongside the other aerial flycatchers. These vivid birds brighten any day, though I begrudge them taking away so much of the trouts' staple diet.

There's one more group of small birds that lifts my spirits. Thrushes, except for the ubiquitous robin, are plain enough brown birds, but they're lovely singers. They nest close to my house—I was careful to cut down as few trees as possible—and their flutelike notes orchestrate sunrises and sunsets. Veeries and song thrushes have strong, clear, characteristic voices, but the hermit thrush knows the best tune.

Several woodpeckers spiral up the tree trunks in front of my house, mostly hairys and downys, but the spectacular pileated occasionally shows up, too. All act like mechanical toys and their cackling calls make me suspect they're not playing with a full deck. Flickers, which are numerous, spend most of their time sensibly pecking up ants from the gravelly road-margins, but their raucous calls make me suspicious of them, too.

Still, these flickers may be the sanest of the woodpeckers. At least they head south in the fall, while the rest remain to freeze their bills off.

Hawks and songbirds fly south, too. Some of the eagles stay. Grouse, crows, and the few owls, which I seldom see, also hang around.

Our most common winter birds are small and drab: chickadees, tufted titmice, juncos, nuthatches, and brown creepers. But then, gaudy birds might seem out of place during this period of mourning for the departed year.

21

The Once and Future River

Unquestionably, it is the geology of our region that has exerted the dominant influence on nearly all aspects of the history of the Neversink Valley. It was the cooling altitude of the Catskills and their thin, infertile topsoils that dictated the original vegetation. Shallow-rooted, acid-tolerant hemlocks dominated the primeval forests. When these virgin stands had been removed, human populations remained sparse because the major nineteenth century livelihood, subsistence farming, was marginal here.

The composition of the rock strata, the soils made up from them, and the mulch from the trees the soil nurtured mandated the quality of water that would flow down its river. This, in turn, limited the types and populations of fish that could or would inhabit it.

The brook trout of the Northeast and eastern Canada—and Atlantic salmon, too—have the rare ability to thrive in acidic water. Since most of the original range of these two salmonids lay in infertile and often highly acidic territory, they either evolved to exploit their nutrient-poor environment or adapted to its conditions. From all reports, the early nineteenth century Neversink literally teemed with brook trout, even though its waters must have been even more acidic than they are now.

The river we fish today is quite different from the one white men first encountered. It is wider, shallower, and warmer than it used to be. Both its floods and its droughts are more severe, too. It still holds good populations of brookies, but probably nothing like the numbers that once swarmed in its clear waters.

What the Neversink of the future will be like is anybody's guess. My own hunch is that the river will continue to recover and improve slightly if present trends are any indication. I think our wild fish will keep on providing *quality* fishing, though I don't foresee a major increase in the *quantity* of it.

Obviously, the number of people living in the drainage basin is going to increase, but not by leaps and bounds. Most of the mountain acreage is owned by the state and can't be built on. Much of the Valley floor and lower elevations are tied up in large estates where new building will be minimal. Then, too, the New York City Bureau of Water Supply is about to impose restrictions on development and stricter new standards on sewage systems on all lands that drain into its reservoirs. Exactly how draconian these regulations will be is still under discussion, but they are certain to discourage attempts to construct new, high-density developments.

With this gradual increase in inhabitants will come more gardens, more saddle horses, and probably more livestock, too, since many ex-urbanites try to live the true country life. All these activities, including effluent from their wastes, no matter how scrupulously it is treated, will add fertility to the water. Even its pH might edge up a notch.

How all this will affect the fishery is hard to predict with any certainty. I would expect the brown trout to respond favorably to any increases in nutrients and pH, but I'm not so sure it will do much for the brook trout. More and bigger browns would take over more of the lies and a larger share of the food. Then too, brookies are an acid-loving, or at least acid-tolerant, species that might gain nothing from an upward creep in pH.

The same is probably true for the landlocked salmon. The number of smolts produced in the river—as opposed to the three thousand usually stocked into the reservoir each year—seems to be increasing, and we estimate that between 20 and 30 percent of all the adult salmon now being caught are un-fin-clipped, river-bred fish. How a slightly richer water supply would affect production of samlets is a tough one to call.

I expect water temperatures to stay about where they are. The limited acreage of land that may be cleared for new dwellings, and therefore subject to increased solar heat-up, should be offset by a denser overstory as forests continue to mature. If or when they agree that global warming is a reality, I'd have to change this estimate.

An additional source of nutrients for the river should come from the hardwood forests. Each autumn, their leaf-fall on hills, mountains, and flatlands lays down another layer of mulch. This should increase buffering of the acidic rainwater and add organic nutrients, too, but the rate of increase will, of course, be snaillike and hardly noticeable in a lifetime. Depending on forestry practices, the woods may gradually revert back to the original hemlock climax with its acidifying effect, but I can't see that happening in the next few hundred years.

Riverbanks should tighten up in the years ahead, pinching flows in floodtime and scouring the bed down to larger, fish-holding and fish-hiding rocks. In the last few years, several eroding banks have been solidly riprapped. This was undertaken mainly to protect roadways and houses, but the benefits to the river and the fishery are undeniable. Several deflectors have been installed recently for purely fishy reasons.

Bankside trees are getting more attention, too. Undermined, lean-ing trees are usually cut down by property owners, and their trunks cut up into harmless six-foot sections. This takes the leverage off the stump and rootball, which will then usually stay put through subsequent floods, anchoring the bank. Replacement trees are springing up in these more stable margins. Some years, when the streambed is heavily littered with downed trees, a collection is taken up to saw up these potential battering rams.

Overall, riparian owners are increasingly aware of the importance of their stretches of river, and are doing more to protect and improve their water. They're realizing that not only are they "not making any more of it," but that they're not selling any more of it either. I can recall only two short pieces, too small to be considered fisheries, that have changed hands in the last twenty years.

I can't claim any credit for this increased concern despite my occasional preachings on the benefits of habitat improvement. The scarcity of for-sale private water, and the increasing traffic on public fisheries, have convinced people that having a blue-ribbon fishery so close to New York City is a nearly priceless asset.

I was recently asked, "If you had it to do all over again, would you undertake the same experiments and improvement programs?" The answer is generally yes, with a few reservations and modifications. Of course I wouldn't think of wasting time and sweat on that Mickey Mouse dam I put in during my first season. And I certainly wouldn't truck in limestone again, knowing what I do now about the power of floodwaters, though it seemed a wizard idea at the time. I'll plead guilty to ignorance, but not to stupidity.

I would probably build the same structures in much the same places, but I might use different construction methods. My first two deflectors, both log cribbings, were filled by the Chinese-coolie method—one rock at a time. This delayed their completion, putting the partly finished structures at risk to floods, and was very likely economically unproductive as well. I was probably working for less than fifty cents an hour, and no matter how little I get paid for my writing, I should be doing better than that. There are some strong teenagers around who are willing to work for the minimum wage, and I should have brought a couple of them in. Perhaps machinery, despite its seemingly high hourly cost, would be the best deal. I am continually amazed at the amount of rock and gravel a fair-sized front-end loader can dig up and transport in sixty minutes.

I might have used different materials on my last structure—the triangle-shaped all-rock deflector just above and opposite my lower cribbing. Because they offer overhead protection for trout throughout their entire lengths, log cribbings seem to hold more fish than rock structures do. As to the Great Wall, I had no choice but to use huge rocks.

Minor improvement efforts such as anchoring evergreens in pools and teeing up rock slabs are worthwhile, I feel, even though they last only a season—if that. They take only minutes to complete, and if they hold a few extra trout that's time well spent.

A more important question that I often ask myself is, What have been the net gains from these various efforts? To the river as a whole, I'll have to admit, there has been little benefit. After all, I've been tinkering with less than 5 percent of the river system.

They have considerably improved my short stretch of water, though. The instream structures now hold more and larger trout than before. I can usually raise two or three browns over a foot long at each forty-foot cribbing. I have raised as many as six on especially good evenings, and I'm not sure there weren't even more that just wouldn't show. Remember, this was previously unproductive water. I'm also convinced that trout overwinter in some of them, making early-spring fishing far more productive than before.

The weed in the pond is a distinct success, even though it has failed to spread into and establish itself in the river proper. The food factory it supports in the pond doesn't benefit the river, either, but a lot of the extra brook trout it produces do find their way into the stream and they certainly enhance the fishery.

About the merits of feeding lights, I have no doubts. My brookies average bigger and fatter than they do in other sections of river. Browns have to benefit from this extra food, too. Anyway, well-fed fish tend to stay put and not wander off looking for extra rations. I don't claim that my hundred pounds a year of lungburger is changing the world or even my small corner of it, but it has to put on at least twenty-five pounds of trout flesh each season. If everyone else fed regularly, there'd be hundreds of pounds of wild fish added to the river's inventory each year, but I've given up on that missionary effort.

I like to think that the spawning beds I created have helped the river system, but I have no proof. It's possible that the river doesn't need more fry to stock itself and that I'm only creating a doomed surplus. Still, it can't hurt, and just observing the gunboats on the redds is reward enough for the few hours spent.

The stocking of landlocked salmon, which was not my doing, has so far done little to benefit the river fishery. I can only hope that river-bred smolts will increase in numbers and that more of these imprinted fish will answer the call of their natal river during high water. Good landlock fishing in the river would be a welcome miracle, but right now it seems to be a very long shot.

This may sound paranoid, but I've found that most of the surprises the river has sprung on me have been distinctly unpleasant ones. So it is heartening to report on one project that took an unexpected turn for the better after having been crossed off as a failure.

It has been nearly fifteen years since we put the first, exotic, Canadian brook trout into one of the Queen's ponds and, as you may remember, some two hundred of those Assinicas that were sexually mature escaped into the river in October. Unfortunately, nobody checked that stretch of water during the following month to see whether or not any of the fugitives engaged in redd-cutting. Since all the fish were both fertile and ripe, some must have buried their eggs. Few should have died in their first river month because all were in excellent, plump condition. We know that some even made it through the menacing winter because several were recaptured the following season.

Then, too, I'd planted several batches of the bright-spotted Tamis-camies into the river and connecting waters, and while I caught quite a few of these fin-clipped fish during the year of their stocking, I never captured one that I considered a hold-over from the previous season. All in all, I had crossed off the possibility of establishing a "miracle" strain in the Neversink.

Then, four autumns ago, I saw two large brookies redd-cutting in the riffle at the tail of Junction Pool. Both were about twenty inches long and they were the first ones I'd ever seen spawning in the main-stem river. It seemed reasonable that fish that big wouldn't need to seek out pea-gravel in bogans and brooks the way seven- or eight-inchers do, but were quite capable of moving the golf- to tennis-ball-sized rocks that the browns and salmon did. What puzzled me was where brookies that size had come from. I guessed that they had been sluiced down into the reservoir by some flood, connected with a school of smelt, and had pigged out for a couple of years before returning upriver.

The next season made me rethink that hypothesis. A brook trout of nearly eighteen inches was landed five miles up the West Branch in June. A slightly larger fish spent the month of July under a log in the old Hewitt water just below me. And that October, I saw five or six in my water that measured from eighteen up to nearly twenty-four inches.

Clearly, that first pair of spawning brookies was no one-shot fluke. Each year since then we have observed increasing numbers of these oversized brook trout. Best of all, they're now showing up in late spring and summer as well as during the spawning season.

A few more of them are being caught each season, too. This past year I caught one of nearly two and a half pounds in May. Then, in

June, the biologist took one of over twenty-one inches that weighed four pounds, six ounces. That's a Labrador-sized brookie. While we have no proof, the best guess is that these fish are descendents of that first stocking of Assinicas. They're heavy-bodied fish and lack the huge, bright, Tamiscamie spots. Of course they could be a cross between the two Canadian strains, but they're certainly not the offspring of our indigenous fish. Whatever their ancestry, may their tribe increase.

When I'm away from the Valley, and sometimes when I'm in it, I lull myself to sleep by starting in at the bottom of my water and casting to every known lie on my way upriver. Always, during this fantasy, the water's at perfect fishing level, the sun sparkles off the riffles, and I see fish throwing water. This make-believe is so soothing that I rarely get as far as Cliff Pool before the alarm clock jolts me awake.

Sadly, my fishing diary reminds me that conditions are rarely like this. Memory is the biggest liar in the world—except, perhaps, for a person falling in love. Claryville is no Tucson with day after day of acrylic-blue skies. This is the Northeast and a front predictably pushes through every three days, clouding the sky and usually pelting us with rain. The barometer is low or falling—conditions which almost guarantee indifferent fishing—more often than it is high and still rising. River levels can be too high for wading or too low to travel a fly.

And yet, we do get a few precious days each season when there's not a puff in the sky and the air inhales like menthol. Last year, Saturday, July 7, was like that, and the water was at ideal fishing level, too. At ten-thirty in the morning, I cross the river in front of my house and hurry down the diagonal path to the bottom of my water, but, when I get there, my thermometer tells me I've been too eager. The water is only 58 degrees—it had been a chilly night—and to start in now would only disturb Great Wall Pool and the run that leads into it before the water has reached the sure-taking warmth of 60 degrees.

I force myself to watch warblers and hunt mushrooms for the next forty-five minutes, but my heart isn't in it.

Somehow, I always feel an extra keenness when fishing in the morning. The day is young and crisp and it makes me feel that way, too. I know I'll see few rising fish and that I'm not likely to raise one as big as fourteen inches at that time of day. I'm also aware that I'll have to pass up the deep, slow water that produces so well in the evening, and will have to pound fish up out of fast water. And yet there's extra excitement in fishing this way because each take, when you're prospecting, comes as a sudden surprise. And then there's none of the pressure you tend to feel in the evenings, either, when fish are rising all around you and you feel you ought to be able to catch them. I can't help looking on morning trout as found money.

After an endless period of enforced loitering, I dip my thermometer again and get a reading of 59.5 degrees, which, I convince myself, is really 60 degrees because my instrument always registers a shade lower than my neighbor's. I step in and don't move a fish until I'm well up into the choppy water at the head of the pool, and there I nail a lovely, yellow-bellied brown that stretches to twelve and a half inches and turns out to be the best fish of the morning. In the run along the face of the Great Wall I get a fat brookie that measures an honest ten inches, and just above that, a feisty, nine-inch brown.

I have already taken three decent fish and there's the run into the cribbing, the rock deflector, Cliff Pocket, and the head of Cliff Pool still to come. I stop for a moment on my way upstream to take in the wall of rhododendron blossoms on the far bank, then glance down to watch their reflections dance on the water. And I know then with gut certainty that at this moment of this day that this spot—right here—is the best of all possible places on earth to be.